Workbook 4B

Maths — No Problem!

Singapore Maths
English National Curriculum 2014

Consultant
Dr. Yeap Ban Har

UK Consultant
Dr. Anne Hermanson

Author
Brandon Oh

shinglee

Published by Maths — No Problem!
Copyright © 2016 by Maths — No Problem!

Printed in the United Kingdom
First Printing, 2015
Reprinted in 2016

ISBN 978-1-910504-19-2

Maths — No Problem!
Dowding House, Coach & Horses Passage
Tunbridge Wells, UK TN2 5NP
www.mathsnoproblem.co.uk

Acknowledgements

This Maths — No Problem! series, adapted from the New Syllabus
Primary Mathematics series, is published in collaboration with
Shing Lee Publishers. Pte Ltd. The publisher would like to thank
Dr. Tony Gardiner for his contribution.

Design and Illustration by Kin

Preface

Maths — No Problem! is a comprehensive series that adopts a spiral design with carefully built-up mathematical concepts and processes adapted from the maths mastery approaches used in Singapore. The Concrete-Pictorial-Abstract (C-P-A) approach forms an integral part of the learning process through the materials developed for this series.

Maths — No Problem! incorporates the use of concrete aids and manipulatives, problem-solving and group work.

In Maths — No Problem! Primary 4, these features are exemplified throughout the chapters:

Worksheet

Well-structured exercises which are developed in accordance with the lesson objectives of each chapter.

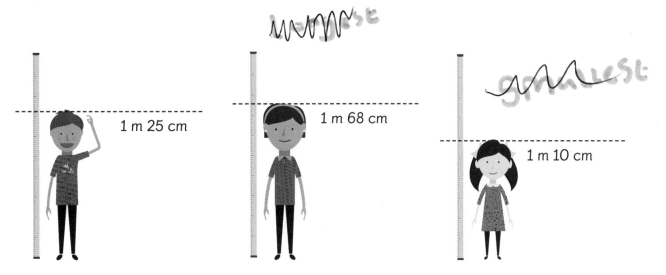

1 m 25 cm

1 m 68 cm

1 m 10 cm

Mind Workout

Higher-order thinking tasks as enrichment for pupils to apply relevant heuristics and extend the concepts and skills learnt.

Review

Follows after each chapter for consolidation of concepts learnt in the chapter.

Revision

Provides an assessment of the consolidation of concepts and skills across strands and topics.

Contents

Decimals

Chapter 8

Name: **Alisha L**   Class: _____   Date: _____

Worksheet 1

Writing Tenths

1   Write the decimal shown by the shaded part.

(a)

1 tenth = $\dfrac{1}{10}$ = $\boxed{0.1}$

(b)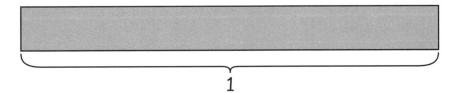

$\square$ tenths = $\square$ = $\square$

(c)

$\square$ tenths = $\square$ = $\square$

(d)

```
▨▨▨▨□□□□□□
```

☐ tenths = ☐ = ☐

(e)

```
▨▨▨▨▨▨▨▨▨□
```

☐ tenths = ☐ = ☐

2 Shade to show each decimal.

```
▨▨▨▨▨▨▨▨▨▨
```
⎨‾‾‾‾‾‾‾‾‾‾‾‾‾‾‾‾‾‾‾‾⎬
            1

(a) 0.2
```
□□□□□□□□□□
```

(b) 0.5
```
□□□□□□□□□□
```

(c) 0.7
```
□□□□□□□□□□
```

(d) 0.6
```
□□□□□□□□□□
```

Name: _____ Class: _____ Date: _____

Writing Tenths

1 Complete each place-value chart and write the decimal shown.

(a)

(0.1)(0.1)(0.1)(0.1)(0.1)

Ones	Tenths
0	5

0 ones + 5 tenths

= 0 + 0.5

= ☐

(b)

(1)(1)(0.1)(0.1)

Ones	Tenths

☐ ones + ☐ tenths

= ☐ + ☐

= ☐

(c)

(1)(1)(1)(0.1)(0.1)
(0.1)(0.1)(0.1)(0.1)

Ones	Tenths

☐ ones + ☐ tenths

= ☐ + ☐

= ☐

(d)

Ones	Tenths
•	

☐ ones + ☐ tenths

= ☐ + ☐

= ☐

2 Fill in the blanks.

(a) **1.3**

The digit 1 stands for ☐ one.

The digit 3 stands for ☐ tenths.

(b) **4.2**

The digit 4 stands for 4 ☐.

The digit 2 stands for 2 ☐.

(c) **6.5**

The digit 6 is in the ☐ place.

The digit 5 is in the ☐ place.

(d) **7.9**

The value of the digit 7 is ☐.

The value of the digit 9 is ☐.

(e) **23.4**

The digit 2 stands for ☐ tens.

The digit 3 stands for ☐ ones.

The digit 4 stands for ☐ tenths.

Worksheet 3

Writing Tenths

1 Fill in the blanks.

(a)　14 tenths　= 10 tenths + 4 tenths

　　　　　　　= 1 one + 4 tenths

　　　　　　　= ☐

(b)　17 tenths　= ☐ tenths + ☐ tenths

　　　　　　　= ☐ one + ☐ tenths

　　　　　　　= ☐

(c)　32 tenths　= ☐ tenths + ☐ tenths

　　　　　　　= ☐ ones + ☐ tenths

　　　　　　　= ☐

(d)　65 tenths　= ☐ tenths + ☐ tenths

　　　　　　　= ☐ one + ☐ tenths

　　　　　　　= ☐

2 Write each number as a decimal.

(a) 3 tenths = ☐

(b) 7 tenths = ☐

(c) 13 tenths = ☐

(d) 27 tenths = ☐

(e) 35 tenths = ☐

(f) $\dfrac{19}{10}$ = ☐

(g) $\dfrac{36}{10}$ = ☐

(h) $\dfrac{91}{10}$ = ☐

3 Fill in the missing decimals.

(a)

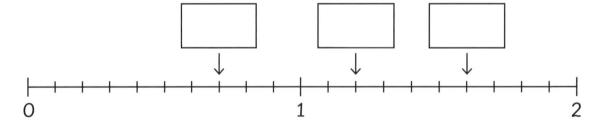

(b)

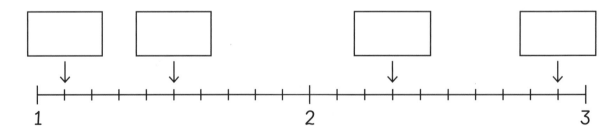

Worksheet 4

Writing Hundredths

1 Write the decimal shown by the shaded part.

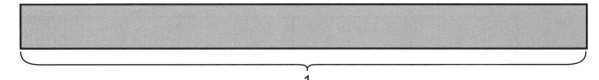

1

(a)

9 hundredths = $\dfrac{9}{100}$ = [ ]

(b)

[ ] hundredths = [ ] = [ ]

(c)

[ ] hundredths = [ ] = [ ]

(d)

[ ] hundredths = [ ] = [ ]

2 Shade to show the decimal.

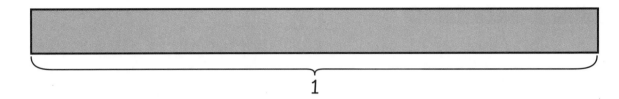

1

(a) 0.05

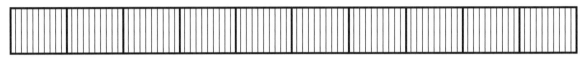

(b) 0.21

(c) 0.36

(d) 0.52

(e) 0.79

Worksheet 5

Writing Hundredths

1 Write the mass shown on each scale in words and in numbers.

(a)

(b)

(c)

(d)

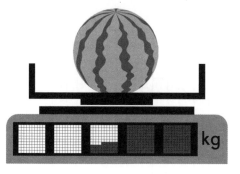

2 Colour to show the decimal.

(a) 1.25

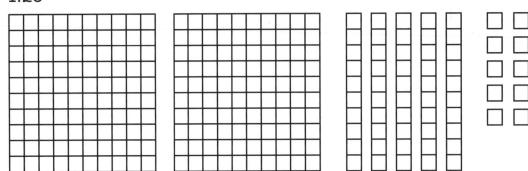

(b) 1.46

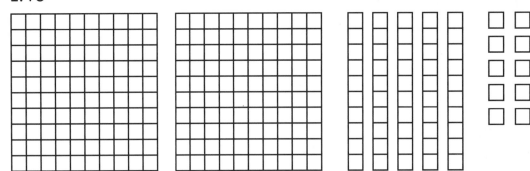

(c) 2.17

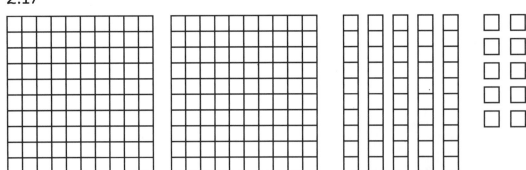

(d) 2.50

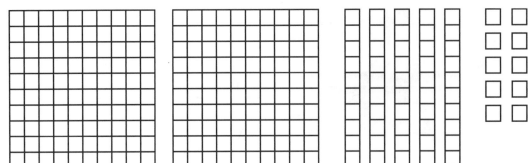

Name: _____ Class: _____ Date: _____

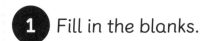

Writing Hundredths

1 Fill in the blanks.

(a)

0.01 0.01 0.01 0.01 0.01 0.01
0.01 0.01 0.01 0.01 0.01 0.01

Ones	Tenths	Hundredths

12 hundredths = 1 tenth + 2 hundredths

= 0.1   + 0.02

= [   ]

(b)

0.01 0.01 0.01 0.01 0.01 0.01
0.01 0.01 0.01 0.01 0.01 0.01
0.01 0.01 0.01 0.01

Ones	Tenths	Hundredths

16 hundredths = [   ] tenths + [   ] hundredths

= [   ] + [   ]

= [   ]

(c)

| 0.01 | 0.01 | 0.01 | 0.01 | 0.01 | 0.01 | 0.01 |

| 0.01 | 0.01 | 0.01 | 0.01 | 0.01 | 0.01 | 0.01 |

| 0.01 | 0.01 | 0.01 | 0.01 | 0.01 | 0.01 | 0.01 |

| 0.01 | 0.01 |

Ones	Tenths	Hundredths
	•	

23 hundredths = [ ] tenths + [ ] hundredths

= [ ] + [ ]

= [ ]

2 Write each number as a decimal.

(a) 4 hundredths = [ ]

(b) 6 hundredths = [ ]

(c) 17 hundredths = [ ]

(d) 53 hundredths = [ ]

(e) 68 hundredths = [ ]

3 Write each number as a decimal.

(a) $\dfrac{7}{100}$ = ☐

(b) $\dfrac{9}{100}$ = ☐

(c) $\dfrac{25}{100}$ = ☐

(d) $\dfrac{81}{100}$ = ☐

(e) $\dfrac{92}{100}$ = ☐

(f) $1\dfrac{3}{100}$ = ☐

(g) $1\dfrac{39}{100}$ = ☐

(h) $2\dfrac{10}{100}$ = ☐

(i) $2\dfrac{77}{100}$ = ☐

(j) $3\dfrac{85}{100}$ = ☐

Worksheet 7

Writing Hundredths

1 Fill in the blanks.

(a)

Ones	Tenths	Hundredths
1	2	5

125 hundredths = 1 one + 2 tenths + 5 hundredths

= 1 + 0.2 + 0.05

= ☐

(b)

Ones	Tenths	Hundredths

139 hundredths = ☐ one + ☐ tenths + ☐ hundredths

= ☐ + ☐ + ☐

= ☐

(c)

Ones	Tenths	Hundredths

374 hundredths = ☐ ones + ☐ tenths + ☐ hundredths

= ☐ + ☐ + ☐

= ☐

2 Write each number as a decimal.

(a) 143 hundredths = [ ]

(b) 269 hundredths = [ ]

(c) 307 hundredths = [ ]

(d) 560 hundredths = [ ]

(e) $\dfrac{107}{100}$ = [ ]

(f) $\dfrac{253}{100}$ = [ ]

(g) $\dfrac{599}{100}$ = [ ]

3 Fill in the missing decimals.

(a)

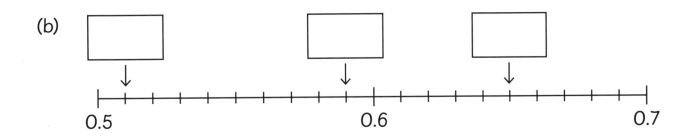

(b)

Worksheet 8

Writing Decimals

1 What does the digit 9 stand for in each number?

(a)   0.89 [   ]   (b)   7.98 [   ]

(c)   9.27 [   ]   (d)   98.16 [   ]

2 Match. What does the digit 4 stand for in each number?

27.46 •

26.74 •

42.67 •

• $\dfrac{4}{100}$

• 40

• 4

• $\dfrac{4}{10}$

3 Fill in the blanks.

Tens	Ones	Tenths	Hundredths
5	0	9	7

(a)   The digit 7 stands for [   ].

(b)   The digit 9 stands for [   ].

Worksheet 9

Comparing and Ordering Decimals

1 Circle the greatest number in each box.

| (a) | 0.3 | 0.6 | 0.7 | 0.4 |

| (b) | 0.45 | 0.25 | 0.35 | 0.15 |

| (c) | 0.09 | 0.8 | 0.07 | 0.7 |

| (d) | 0.67 | 0.7 | 0.6 | 0.76 |

2 Circle the smallest number in each box.

| (a) | 0.9 | 0.5 | 0.6 | 0.3 |

| (b) | 0.17 | 0.07 | 0.01 | 0.2 |

| (c) | 0.02 | 0.1 | 0.37 | 0.27 |

| (d) | 0.3 | 0.33 | 0.13 | 0.03 |

3 Fill in the blanks with > or <.

(a) 0.4 ☐ 0.5

(b) 0.09 ☐ 0.08

(c) 0.21 ☐ 0.12

(d) 0.56 ☐ 0.55

(e) 0.62 ☐ 0.67

(f) 0.90 ☐ 0.88

4 Arrange the numbers in increasing order.

| 0.82 | 0.8 | 0.88 | 0.28 |

☐ , ☐ , ☐ , ☐

5 Arrange the numbers in decreasing order.

| 0.97 | 0.79 | 0.7 | 0.9 |

☐ , ☐ , ☐ , ☐

Worksheet 10

Comparing and Ordering Decimals

1 Circle the greatest number in each box.

(a)

| 2.3 | 1.2 | 3.2 | 1.3 |

(b)

| 2.62 | 2.64 | 2.59 | 2.65 |

(c)

| 1.78 | 1.8 | 1.7 | 1.08 |

2 Circle the smallest number in each box.

(a)

| 1.4 | 1.5 | 1.7 | 1.6 |

(b)

| 9.09 | 7.07 | 6.06 | 8.08 |

(c)

| 3.42 | 3.47 | 3.43 | 3.5 |

3 Fill in the blanks with > or <.

(a) 1.43 ☐ 1.33

(b) 3.04 ☐ 3.07

(c) 5.88 ☐ 5.79

(d) 8.49 ☐ 8.5

(e) 7.1 ☐ 7.01

4 Arrange the numbers in increasing order.

| 1.45 | 1.5 | 1.54 | 1.4 |

☐ , ☐ , ☐ , ☐

5 Arrange the numbers in decreasing order.

| 5.98 | 9.58 | 8.95 | 9.85 |

☐ , ☐ , ☐ , ☐

Worksheet 11

Comparing and Ordering Decimals

1 Circle the greatest number and cross out the smallest number in each box.

(a)

| 12.6 | 13.2 | 12.3 | 13.6 |

(b)

| 10.37 | 12.37 | 10.35 | 12.35 |

(c)

| 16.05 | 10.5 | 16.5 | 10.65 |

(d)

| 34.92 | 36.7 | 32.48 | 30.79 |

(e)

| 44.2 | 22.4 | 42.4 | 24.4 |

2 Fill in the blanks with > or <.

(a) 12.4 [ ] 21.2

(b) 13.57 [ ] 13.59

(c) 22.32 [ ] 22.23

(d) 30.03 [ ] 30.13

(e) 54.6 [ ] 54.61

3 Fill in the place-value chart. Arrange the numbers in increasing order.

| 23.45 | 32.54 | 24.35 | 32.45 |

Tens	Ones	Tenths	Hundredths

☐ , ☐ , ☐ , ☐

4 Fill in the place-value chart. Arrange the numbers in decreasing order.

| 76.18 | 76.1 | 67.81 | 67.8 |

Tens	Ones	Tenths	Hundredths

☐ , ☐ , ☐ , ☐

Name: _____ Class: _____ Date: _____

Worksheet 12

Making Number Patterns

1 Continue each number pattern.

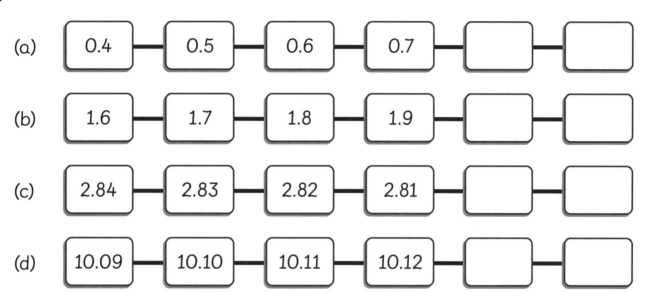

(a) 0.4 — 0.5 — 0.6 — 0.7 — ☐ — ☐

(b) 1.6 — 1.7 — 1.8 — 1.9 — ☐ — ☐

(c) 2.84 — 2.83 — 2.82 — 2.81 — ☐ — ☐

(d) 10.09 — 10.10 — 10.11 — 10.12 — ☐ — ☐

2 Fill in the missing numbers in each number pattern.

(a) 6.7 6.8 6.9 7.0 ◯ ◯ 7.3 ◯

(b) ◯ 9.8 9.7 ◯ 9.5 ◯ 9.3 ◯

(c) 8.46 8.47 ◯ 8.49 ◯ ◯ 8.52 8.53

(d) 15.89 ◯ 15.91 15.92 ◯ 15.94 15.95 ◯

3 Fill in the blanks.

    (a)   What number is 0.1 less than 8.5?

                                                                         [   ]

    (b)   What number is 0.01 more than 3.14?

                                                                         [   ]

4 Fill in the blanks.

    (a)   0.1 more than 0.9 is [   ].

    (b)   0.01 less than 1.45 is [   ].

    (c)   0.1 less than 2.2 is [   ].

    (d)   0.01 more than 4.78 is [   ].

    (e)   0.1 more than 17.4 is [   ].

    (f)   0.01 less than 20.98 is [   ].

    (g)   0.1 less than 33.3 is [   ].

    (h)   0.01 more than 48.95 is [   ].

Name: _____ Class: _____ Date: _____

Worksheet 13

Rounding Decimals

1 Express each measurement as a fraction and as a decimal.

(a)

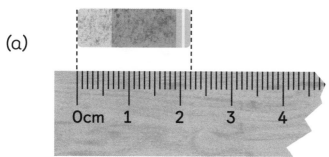

The length of the rubber is 2 $\dfrac{\boxed{}}{10}$ cm or $\boxed{}$ cm.

(b)

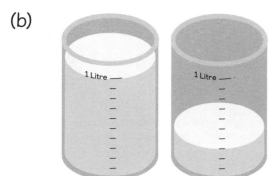

The volume of water is 1 $\dfrac{\boxed{}}{10}$ l or $\boxed{}$ l.

(c)

3.8 kg

The mass of the pineapple is 3 $\dfrac{\boxed{}}{10}$ kg or $\boxed{}$ kg.

2 Round each measurement to the nearest whole number.

(a)

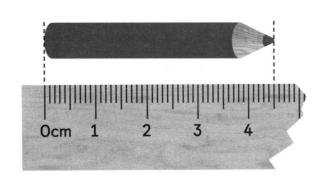

The length of the pencil is 4.5 cm.

$4.5 \approx$ ▢

(b)

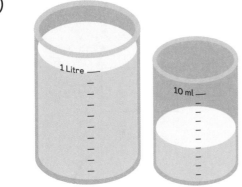

The total volume of water is ▢ l.

▢ $\approx$ ▢

(c)

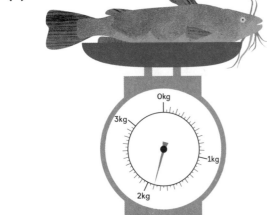

The mass of the fish is ▢ kg.

▢ $\approx$ ▢

Worksheet 14

Rounding Decimals

1 Round each measurement to the nearest cm.

(a)

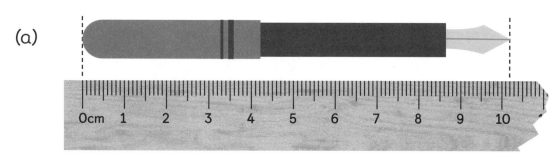

10.2 cm $\approx$ ⬚ cm

(b)

⬚ cm $\approx$ ⬚ cm

(c)

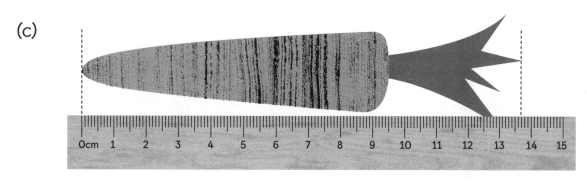

⬚ cm $\approx$ ⬚ cm

2 Record each reading to the nearest kg.

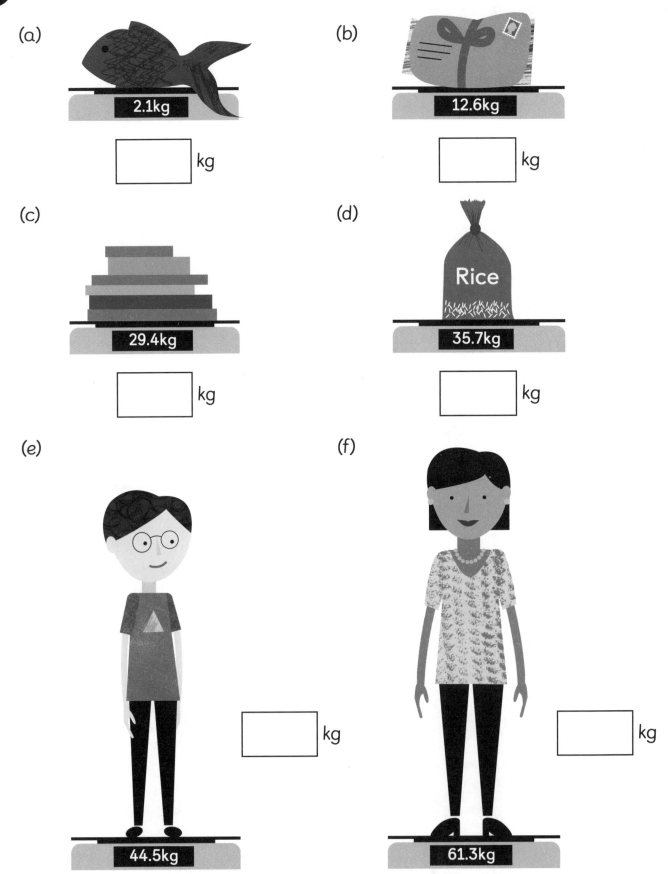

(a) 2.1kg ☐ kg

(b) 12.6kg ☐ kg

(c) 29.4kg ☐ kg

(d) Rice 35.7kg ☐ kg

(e) ☐ kg 44.5kg

(f) ☐ kg 61.3kg

Name: _____ Class: _____ Date: _____

Worksheet 15

Writing Fractions as Decimals

1 Write each fraction as a decimal.

(a) $\dfrac{3}{10}$ = [3] tenths = [0.3]

(b) $\dfrac{9}{10}$ = [ ] tenths = [ ]

(c) $\dfrac{7}{100}$ = [ ] hundredths = [ ]

(d) $\dfrac{23}{100}$ = [ ] hundredths = [ ]

2 Fill in the blanks.

(a) $\dfrac{1}{2}$ = $\dfrac{\Box}{10}$ = [ ] tenths = [ ]

(b) $\dfrac{4}{5}$ = $\dfrac{\Box}{10}$ = [ ] tenths = [ ]

(c) $\dfrac{1}{4}$ = $\dfrac{\Box}{100}$ = [ ] hundredths = [ ]

(d) $\dfrac{3}{25}$ = $\dfrac{\Box}{100}$ = [ ] hundredths = [ ]

(e) $\dfrac{11}{20}$ = $\dfrac{\Box}{100}$ = [ ] hundredths = [ ]

(f) $\dfrac{1}{50}$ = $\dfrac{\Box}{100}$ = [ ] hundredths = [ ]

3 Write each quantity as a decimal.

(a)

$3\frac{3}{4}$ l

[ ] l

(b)

$5\frac{1}{5}$ kg

[ ] kg

(c)

$2\frac{1}{2}$ m

[ ] m

(d)

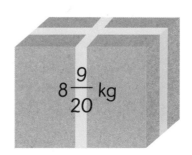

$8\frac{9}{20}$ kg

[ ] kg

4 Match.

1.4 •

1.6 •

• $1\frac{3}{5}$

• $1\frac{9}{20}$

• $1\frac{2}{5}$

Name: _____ Class: _____ Date: _____

Worksheet 16

Dividing Whole Numbers by 10

1 Fill in the blanks.

(a) $1 \div 10 = \boxed{1}$ tenth $= \boxed{0.1}$

(b) $4 \div 10 = \boxed{}$ tenths $= \boxed{}$

(c) $7 \div 10 = \boxed{}$ tenths $= \boxed{}$

(d) $18 \div 10 = \boxed{}$ one $\boxed{}$ tenths $= \boxed{}$

(e) $34 \div 10 = \boxed{}$ ones $\boxed{}$ tenths $= \boxed{}$

(f) $58 \div 10 = \boxed{}$ ones $\boxed{}$ tenths $= \boxed{}$

(g) $97 \div 10 = \boxed{}$ ones $\boxed{}$ tenths $= \boxed{}$

2 This is how Hannah divides.

$14 \div 10 = \boxed{?}$

$14 \div 10 = 1.4$

14 → 10, 4

$$10 \div 10 = 1$$
$$4 \div 10 = 0.4$$
$$\overline{14 \div 10 = 1.4}$$

Use 's method to divide.

(a) $29 \div 10 =$ ☐

$$20 \div 10 = \boxed{}$$

$$9 \div 10 = \boxed{}$$

$$29 \div 10 = \boxed{}$$

(b) $54 \div 10 =$ ☐

$$50 \div 10 = \boxed{}$$

$$4 \div 10 = \boxed{}$$

$$54 \div 10 = \boxed{}$$

(c) $73 \div 10 =$ ☐

$$70 \div 10 = \boxed{}$$

$$3 \div 10 = \boxed{}$$

$$73 \div 10 = \boxed{}$$

(d) $91 \div 10 =$ ☐

$$90 \div 10 = \boxed{}$$

$$1 \div 10 = \boxed{}$$

$$91 \div 10 = \boxed{}$$

Worksheet 17

Dividing Whole Numbers by 100

1 Fill in the blanks.

(a) $2 \div 100$ = [   ] hundredths = [   ]

(b) $5 \div 100$ = [   ] hundredths = [   ]

(c) $9 \div 100$ = [   ] hundredths = [   ]

(d) $30 \div 100$ = [   ] tenths = [   ]

(e) $48 \div 100$ = [   ] tenths [   ] hundredths

= [   ]

(f) $94 \div 100$ = [   ] tenths [   ] hundredths

= [   ]

(g) $354 \div 100$ = [   ] ones [   ] tenths [   ] hundredths

= [   ]

2 Charles divides 18 by 100 this way:

$18 \div 100 = \boxed{?}$

18
/ \
10   8

$10 \div 100 = 0.1$
$8 \div 100 = 0.08$
$18 \div 100 = 0.18$

$18 \div 100 = 0.18$

Use 's method to divide.

(a) $36 \div 100 = \boxed{}$

$30 \div 100 = \boxed{}$

$6 \div 100 = \boxed{}$

$36 \div 100 = \boxed{}$

(b) $64 \div 100 = \boxed{}$

$60 \div 100 = \boxed{}$

$4 \div 100 = \boxed{}$

$64 \div 100 = \boxed{}$

(c) $89 \div 100 = \boxed{}$

$80 \div 100 = \boxed{}$

$9 \div 100 = \boxed{}$

$89 \div 100 = \boxed{}$

3 Divide.

(a) $6 \div 10$ =   ☐

     $6 \div 100$ =   ☐

(b) $7 \div 10$ =   ☐

     $7 \div 100$ =   ☐

(c) $20 \div 10$ =   ☐

     $20 \div 100$ =   ☐

(d) $64 \div 10$ =   ☐

     $64 \div 100$ =   ☐

(e) $89 \div 10$ =   ☐

     $89 \div 100$ =   ☐

Date: _____

Amira used three of the number cards to make a decimal. The decimal is 50, rounded to the nearest whole number.

| 1 | 2 | 3 | 4 | 5 | 6 | 7 | 8 | 9 | 0 |

Write down all the possible decimals that Amira made.

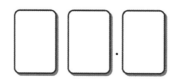

Name: _____ Class: _____ Date: _____

Review 8

1 Complete each place-value chart and write the decimal shown.

(a)

Ones	Tenths
•	

2 ones + 3 tenths = ☐ tenths

(b)
0.1 0.1 0.1 0.1 0.1

0.1 0.1 0.01 0.01

Tenths	Hundredths

7 tenths + 2 hundredths = ☐ hundredths

☐

2 Fill in the blanks.

(a)
25.46

The digit is in the tenths place.

The digit 6 is in the ☐ place.

(b)
82.39

The digit ☐ stands for $\frac{3}{10}$.

The digit 9 stands for ☐.

3 Arrange the numbers in increasing order.

| 5.76 | 5.6 | 5.67 | 5.7 |

[ ] , [ ] , [ ] , [ ]

4 Arrange the numbers in decreasing order.

| 98.8 | 98.98 | 98.89 | 98.9 |

[ ] , [ ] , [ ] , [ ]

5 Fill in the blanks.

(a)　6.3 is 0.1 less than [ ] .

(b)　8.64 is 0.01 more than [ ] .

(c)　[ ] is 0.01 less than 9.37.

(d)　0.1 more than 46.45 is [ ] .

6 Fill in the blanks.

0.1 more than the number is ⬚ .

0.01 less than the number is ⬚ .

1.29

⬚ is 0.1 less than the number.

⬚ is 0.01 more than the number.

7 Write each quantity as a fraction and as a decimal. Round the decimal to the nearest whole number.

(a)

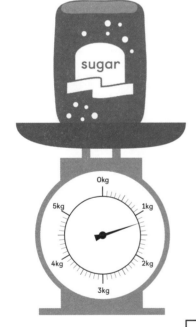

The sugar weighs 1 $\dfrac{\square}{10}$ kg or ⬚ kg.

⬚ ≈ ⬚

(b)

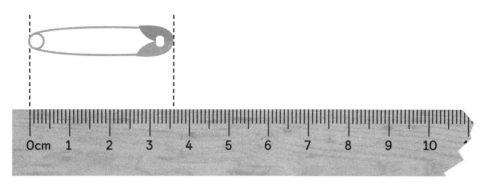

The safety pin is 3 □/10 cm or □ cm long.

□ ≈ □

(c)

The bar of chocolate is 8 □/10 cm or □ cm long.

□ ≈ □

8 Divide.

(a) $3 \div 10 = \boxed{}$ (b) $5 \div 10 = \boxed{}$

(c) $34 \div 10 = \boxed{}$ (d) $56 \div 10 = \boxed{}$

(e) $27 \div 100 = \boxed{}$ (f) $67 \div 100 = \boxed{}$

9 Match.

| 6.1 | ● | ● | $6\dfrac{3}{5}$ |

| 6.6 | ● | ● | $6\dfrac{1}{4}$ |

| 6.25 | ● | ● | $6\dfrac{4}{25}$ |

| 6.16 | ● | ● | $6\dfrac{1}{10}$ |

10 Write in decimals.

(a) $1\frac{2}{5}$ =

(b) $2\frac{8}{50}$ =

(c) $4\frac{3}{25}$ =

(d) $5\frac{15}{20}$ =

11 What are the next four numbers in each of the number patterns?

(a) 2.8, 2.9, 3.0, ☐ , ☐ , ☐ , ☐

(b) 8.5, 8.4, 8.3, ☐ , ☐ , ☐ , ☐

(c) 6.02, 6.03, 6.04, ☐ , ☐ , ☐ , ☐

(d) 2.78, 2.77, 2.76, ☐ , ☐ , ☐ , ☐

Money

Chapter 9

Name: _____ Class: _____ Date: _____

Worksheet 1

Writing Amounts of Money

1

£1

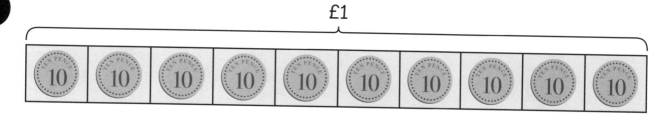

Write the amount of money in £.

(a) 20 10 10 £ [　　]

(b) 50 20 10 £ [　　]

(c) £1 20 20 10 £ [　　]

(d) £1 £1 £1 50 20 £ [　　]

(e)   £ [　　]

2 Circle the coins which make up the correct amount.

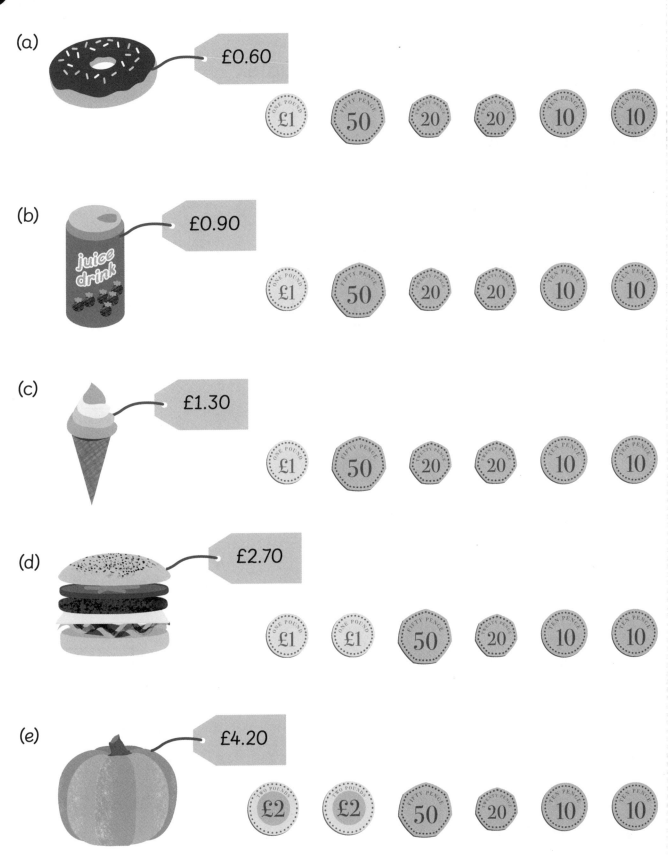

(a) £0.60

(b) £0.90

(c) £1.30

(d) £2.70

(e) £4.20

Worksheet 2

Writing Amounts of Money

1 Write the amount of money in £.

(a)   £ [   ]

(b)  £ [   ]

(c)   £ [   ]

(d)  £ [   ]

2 Match.

£0.48 ●   ● £ 1 and 35 p

£1.35 ●   ● £ 2 and 9 p

£2.09 ●   ● 48 p

3 Circle the coins which make up the correct amount.

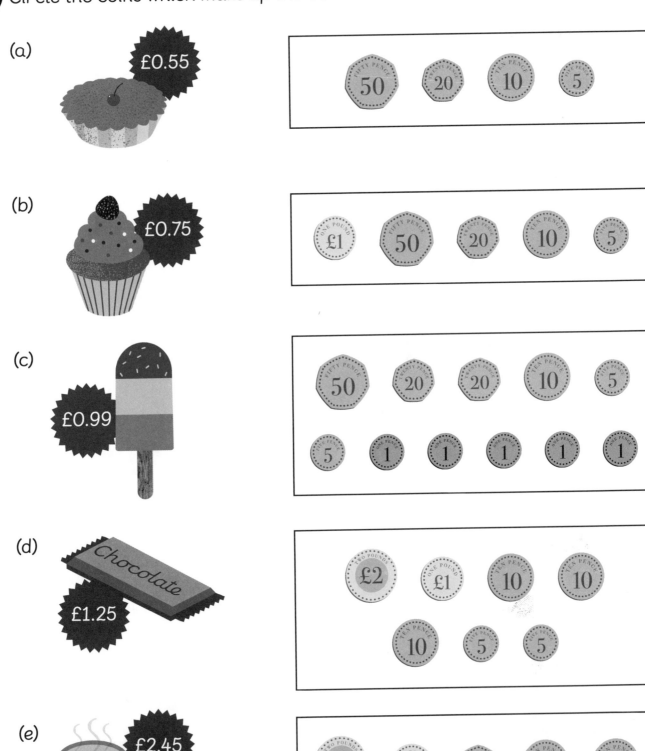

(a) £0.55

50 20 10 5

(b) £0.75

£1 50 20 10 5

(c) £0.99

50 20 20 10 5
5 1 1 1 1 1

(d) £1.25

£2 £1 10 10
10 5 5

(e) £2.45

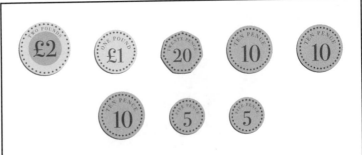

£2 £1 20 10 10
10 5 5

Name: _____ Class: _____ Date: _____

Worksheet 3

Comparing Amounts of Money

1 Write each amount of money in £, then compare the two amounts.

(a)

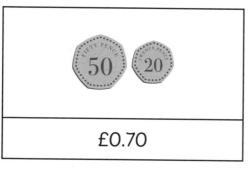

£0.70   £0.60

£ [ ] is more than £ [ ] .

(b)

£ [ ] is less than £ [ ] .

(c)

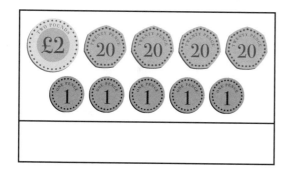

£ [ ] is more than £ [ ] .

Worksheet 4

Rounding Amounts of Money

1 Round each amount to the nearest £.

(a)

£1.60

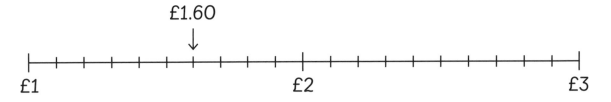

£1.60 ≈ [   ]

(b)

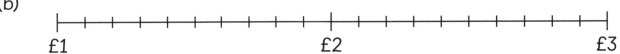

£2.45 ≈ [   ]

(c)

£3.80 ≈ [   ]

(d)

£4.50 ≈ [   ]

2 Round the price of each item to the nearest £ and to the nearest £10.

(a) £15.80

£15.80 ≈ [ ] (to the nearest £)

£15.80 ≈ [ ] (to the nearest £10)

(b) £23.25

£23.25 ≈ [ ] (to the nearest £)

£23.25 ≈ [ ] (to the nearest £10)

(c) £37.90

£37.90 ≈ [ ] (to the nearest £)

£37.90 ≈ [ ] (to the nearest £10)

3 Complete the table.

	Round to the nearest £	Round to the nearest £10
£9.11		
£12.64		
£15.43		
£28.50		

Worksheet 5

Solving Problems Involving Money

£1.98

£5.75

£6.50

£2.65

£3.29

£7.35

1 Calculate the total cost of each group of fruit.

(a)	
(b)	
(c)	

2 Calculate the change.

(a)

has £10.

He buys  .

His change is £ [____] .

(b)

has £10.

She buys  and  .

Her change is £ [____] .

(c)

has £10.

He buys  and  .

His change is £ [____] .

(d)

has £10.

She buys  and 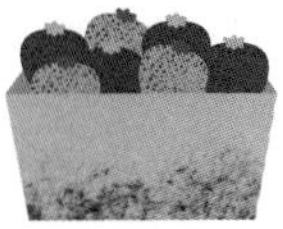 .

Her change is £ [____] .

Worksheet 6

Solving Problems Involving Money

£1.65   £3.06   £1.99   £2.78

1 Calculate the total cost of each.

(a)	
(b)	
(c)	
(d)	

2 Calculate the change.

(a) 👤 has £10.

He buys 🛍️🛍️ .

His change is £ _____ .

(b) 👧 has £10.

She buys 🛍️🛍️ and 🥚 .

Her change is £ _____ .

(c) 👦 has £10.

He buys 🥛🥛 and 🥚🥚 .

His change is £ _____ .

Worksheet 7

Solving Problems Involving Money

Thai House

Total Bill:
£18.36

1 and share the cost of their dinner.

How much does each of them pay if:

(a) they share the cost of their dinner equally?

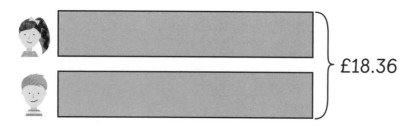

£18.36

(b) pays twice as much as ?

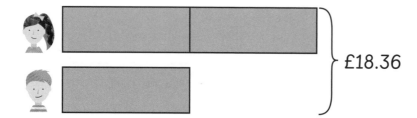

£18.36

(c) pays three times as much as ?

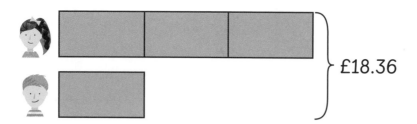

£18.36

2   and share the cost of a present.

How much does each of them pay if:

(a)   they share the cost equally?

(b)    pays twice as much as   ?

(c)    pays 4 times as much as   ?

Worksheet 8

Estimating Amounts of Money

1

Lollies £1.12

£2.05

£1.89

CHOCOLATE £1.73

fruity Sweets £0.28

Estimate the total amount of each group of items by rounding each price to the nearest £.

(a) £ [   ]

(b) £ [   ]

(c) £ [   ]

(d) £ [   ]

(e) £ [   ]

(f) £ [   ]

2

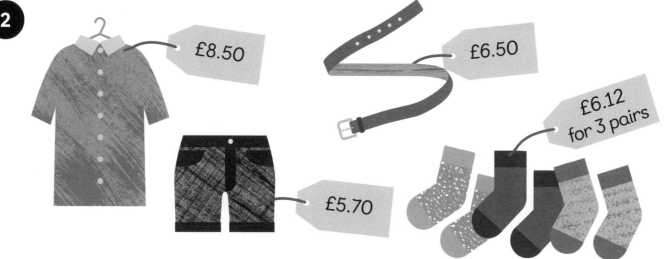

£8.50

£6.50

£6.12 for 3 pairs

£5.70

Estimate the total amount of each group of items by rounding each price to the nearest £10.

(a)  £ [   ]

(b)  £ [   ]

(c)  £ [   ]

(d)  £ [   ]

(e)  £ [   ]

 bought 50 tarts altogether.

She paid £29.70.

How many of each tart did she buy?

Review 9

1 Write each amount of money in £.

(a)  £ [   ]

(b) 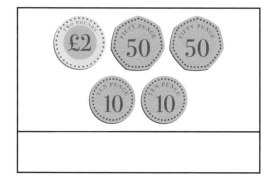 £ [   ]

2 Write each amount of money in £, then compare the two amounts.

(a)

   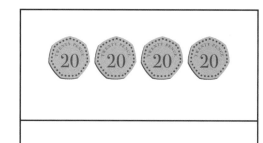

£ [   ] is more than £ [   ] .

(b)

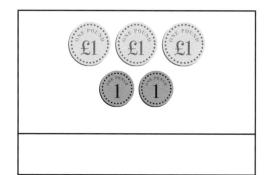

£ [   ] is more than £ [   ] .

3

Round the price of each item to the nearest £ and to the nearest £10.

(a)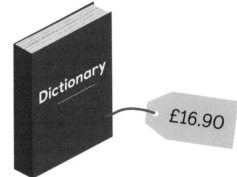

£16.90 ≈ ⬚ (to the nearest £)

£16.90 ≈ ⬚ (to the nearest £10)

(b)

£25.70 ≈ ⬚ (to the nearest £)

£25.70 ≈ ⬚ (to the nearest £10)

(c)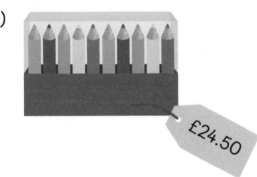

£24.50 ≈ ⬚ (to the nearest £)

£24.50 ≈ ⬚ (to the nearest £10)

(d)

£39.65 ≈ ⬚ (to the nearest £)

£39.65 ≈ ⬚ (to the nearest £10)

4

£3.65

£0.88

£2.49

£2.99

3.65
3.65
7.30

1 1

Find the total cost of each group of items.

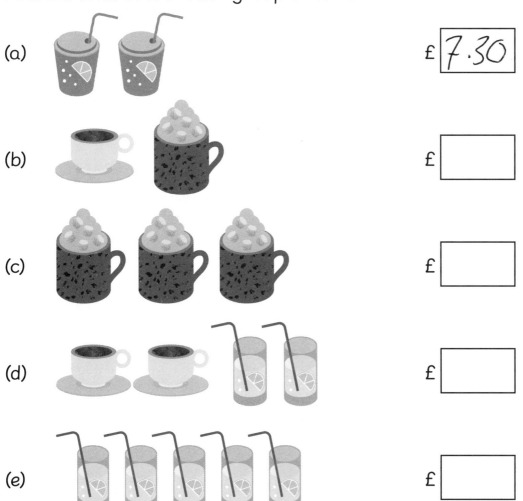

(a) £ 7.30

(b) £

(c) £

(d) £

(e) £

5 Match.

65p x 5 ●	● £3.48
£1.25 x 5 ●	● £7.08
£2.36 x 3 ●	● £3.25
£1.09 x 2 ●	● £6.25
3 x £1.95 ●	● £2.45
49p x 5 ●	● £2.18
	● £5.85

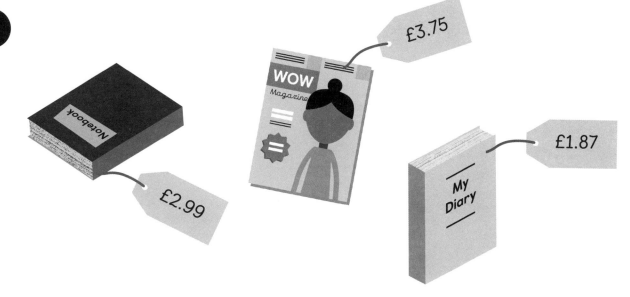

£3.75

£2.99

£1.87

Calculate the expected change.

(a) has £5. He buys and  .

(b) has £7. She buys  and .

(c) has £10. He buys 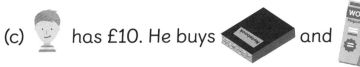 and .

7 Emma has a total of £30 in these two piggy banks.

Find the amount of money in each piggy bank if:

(a)   the ▢▢▢ and 🐷 have the same amount of money.

(b)   the ▢▢▢ has twice as much money as the 🐷.

(c)   the ▢▢▢ has four times as much money as the 🐷.

Mass, Volume and Length

Name: _____ Class: _____ Date: _____

Worksheet 1

Measuring Mass

1 Give the mass of each item to the nearest 0.1 kg.

(a)

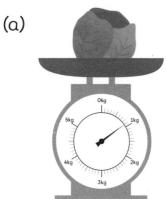

The cabbage weighs about ☐ kg.

(b)

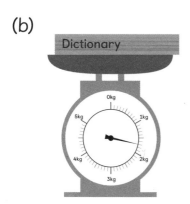

The dictionary weighs about ☐ kg.

(c)

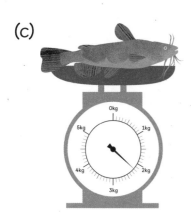

The fish weighs about ☐ kg.

2 Give the mass of each item to the nearest kg.

(a)

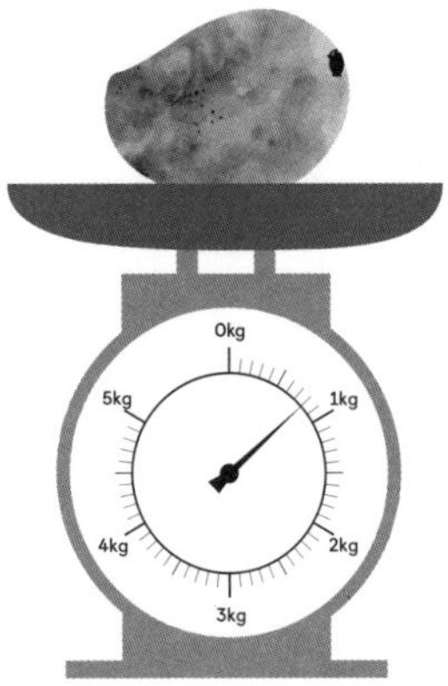

The mango weighs about ☐ kg.

(b)

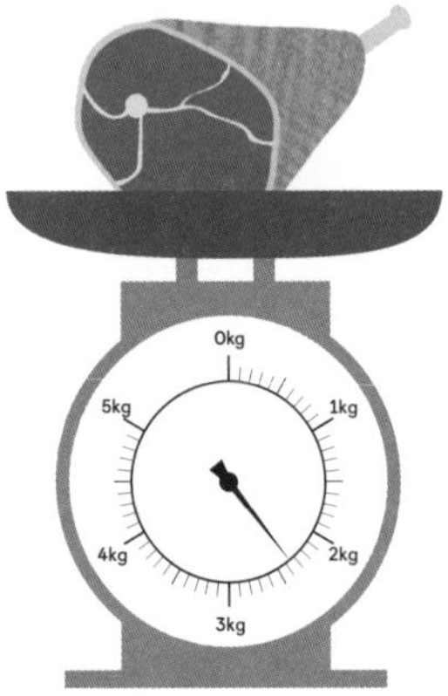

The ham weighs about ☐ kg.

(c)

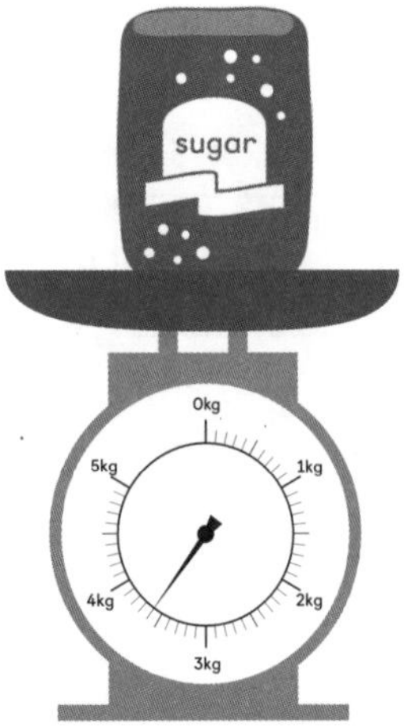

The bag of sugar weighs about ☐ kg.

Name: _____ Class: _____ Date: _____

Worksheet 2

Measuring Mass

1 Find the mass of each item.

(a)

The bag of rice weighs about ☐ kg.

(b)

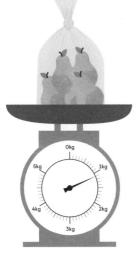

The bag of pears weighs about ☐ kg.

(c)

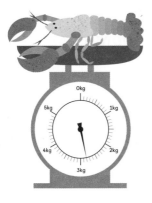

The lobster weighs about ☐ kg.

2 Find the mass of each item. Which item has the same mass as the bag of potatoes?

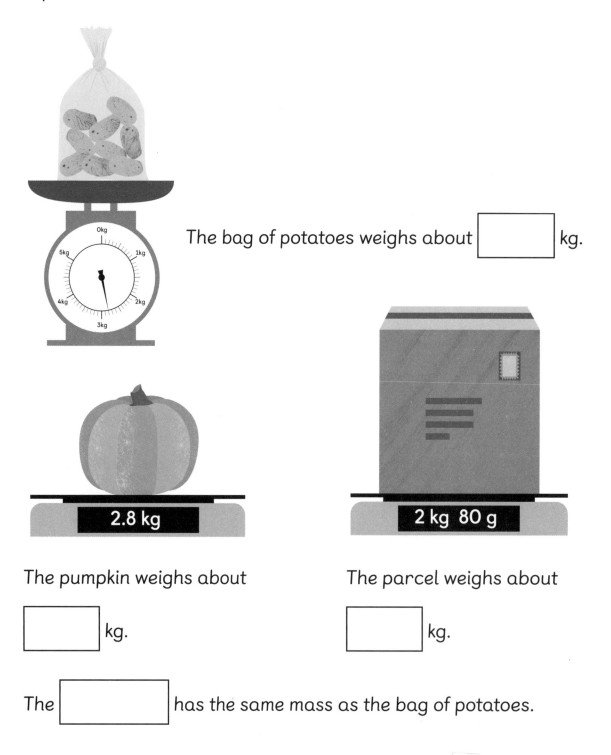

The bag of potatoes weighs about ☐ kg.

The pumpkin weighs about

☐ kg.

The parcel weighs about

☐ kg.

The ☐ has the same mass as the bag of potatoes.

Name: _____ Class: _____ Date: _____

Worksheet 3

Converting Units of Mass

1 Find the mass of each item in g.

(a)

The watermelon weighs ☐ g.

(b)

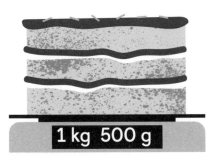

1 kg 500 g

The cake weighs ☐ g.

(c)

2 kg 850 g

The cheese weighs ☐ g.

2 Fill in the blanks.

Sausages
Sausages
Sausages

1 kg 25 g

sausages

1.25 kg

bananas

1205 g

carrots

(a) The mass of the bananas is about ☐ g and the mass of the sausages is ☐ g.

(b) The ☐ are the lightest.

(c) The ☐ are the heaviest.

(d) The mass of the carrots is about ☐ kg, to the nearest 0.1 kg.

(e) Arrange the items, from the lightest to the heaviest.

☐ , ☐ , ☐

Worksheet 4

Measuring Volume

1 Find the volume of water in each measuring cylinder.

(a)

The volume of water in the measuring cylinder is about ⬚ l.

(b)

The volume of water in the measuring cylinder is about ⬚ l.

(c)

The volume of water in the measuring cylinder is about ⬚ l.

2 The water from each container is poured into a measuring cylinder.
By drawing it, show the water level in each measuring cylinder.

(a)

1 Litre

(b)

 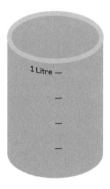

1 Litre

(c)

 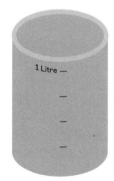

1 Litre

(d)

1 Litre

Name: _____ Class: _____ Date: _____

Worksheet 5

Measuring Volume

1 Find the volume of water in each measuring cylinder.

(a)

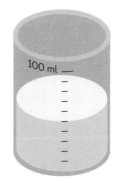

100 ml —

The volume of water in the measuring

cylinder is [   ] l.

(b)

100 ml —

The volume of water in the measuring

cylinder is [   ] l.

(c)

100 ml —

The volume of water in the measuring

cylinder is [   ] l.

(d)

100 ml —

The volume of water in the measuring

cylinder is [   ] l.

2 Find the volume of water in each measuring cylinder.

(a)

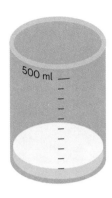

The volume of water in the measuring

cylinder is [   ] l.

(b)

The volume of water in the measuring

cylinder is [   ] l.

(c)

The volume of water in the measuring

cylinder is [   ] l.

(d)

The volume of water in the measuring

cylinder is [   ] l.

Worksheet 6

Converting Units of Volume

1 What is the volume of liquid in each bottle in ml?

(a)

The volume of liquid in the

bottle is about [   ] ml.

(b)

The volume of liquid in the

bottle is about [   ] ml.

(c)

The volume of liquid in the

bottle is about [   ] ml.

2 Fill in the blanks.

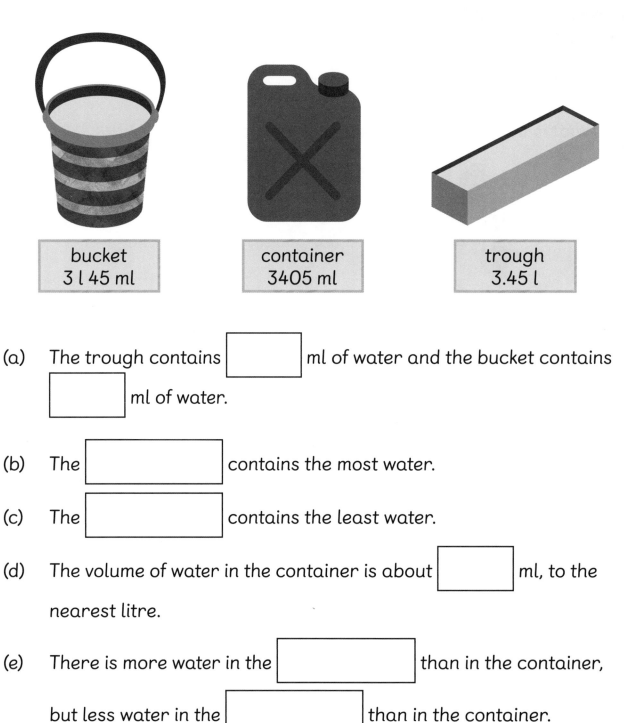

bucket	container	trough
3 l 45 ml	3405 ml	3.45 l

(a) The trough contains [ ] ml of water and the bucket contains [ ] ml of water.

(b) The [ ] contains the most water.

(c) The [ ] contains the least water.

(d) The volume of water in the container is about [ ] ml, to the nearest litre.

(e) There is more water in the [ ] than in the container, but less water in the [ ] than in the container.

Worksheet 7

Measuring Height

1 Find the height of each person.

(a) 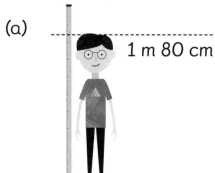 1 m 80 cm

[ ] m

(b)  1 m 25 cm

[ ] m

(c) 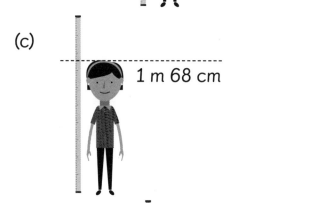 1 m 68 cm

[ ] m

(d)  1 m 10 cm

[ ] m

2 Fill in the blanks.

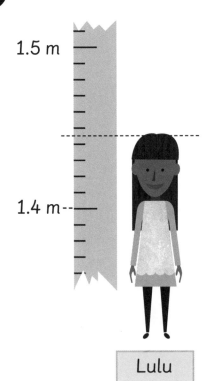

1.5 m

1.4 m

Lulu

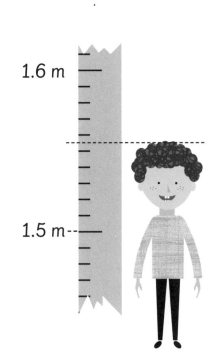

1.6 m

1.5 m

Elliott

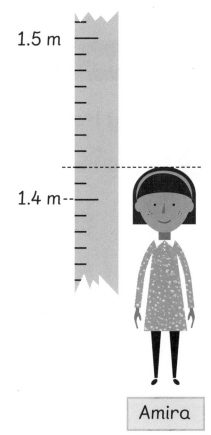

1.5 m

1.4 m

Amira

(a) What is each person's height?

Lulu: ☐ m

Elliott: ☐ m

Amira: ☐ m

(b) ☐ is the tallest.

(c) ☐ is the shortest.

(d) Arrange the children from the shortest to the tallest.

☐ , ☐ , ☐

Worksheet 8

Measuring Length

1 Measure the length of each side of the figure.

(a)

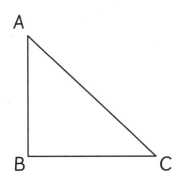

AB = [ ] cm

AC = [ ] cm

BC = [ ] cm

(b)

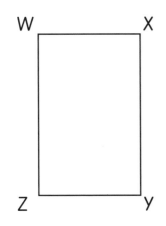

WY = [ ] cm

XY = [ ] cm

ZY = [ ] cm

WZ = [ ] cm

2 Draw.

(a) A rectangle that has a perimeter of about 24 cm.

(b) A triangle that has a perimeter of about 24 cm.

3 Measure each side to the nearest cm and estimate its perimeter.

Perimeter ≈ ⬚ cm

Name: _____ Class: _____ Date: _____

Converting Units of Length

1 Write the length or height of each object in cm.

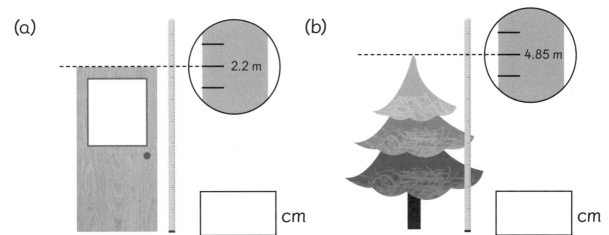

(a)

2.2 m

[ ] cm

(b)

4.85 m

[ ] cm

(c)

8.04 m

[ ] cm

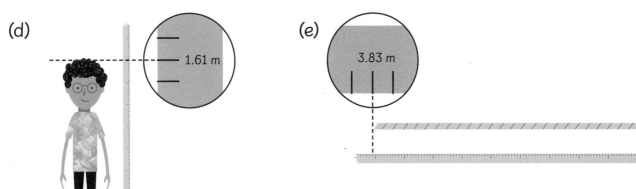

(d)

1.61 m

[ ] cm

(e)

3.83 m

[ ] cm

2 This table shows the distance travelled by each boy's paper plane.

Name	Distance
Ravi	5.02 m
Charles	4.38 m
Sam	6.19 m

(a) What is the distance travelled by each plane?

Ravi's plane: [ ] m [ ] cm

Charles' plane: [ ] m [ ] cm

Sam's plane: [ ] m [ ] cm

(b) Whose plane travelled the furthest?

[ ]

(c) Whose plane travelled a shorter distance than Ravi's plane?

[ ]

(d) Sam's plane travelled [ ] cm further than Charles' plane.

Worksheet 10

Converting Units of Length

1

1.96 km

Library

5.6 km

2.2 km

0.8 km

Restaurant

2.35 km

Market

Write the following distance in metres:

(a) between the playground and the library
         _____ m

(b) between the playground and the restaurant
         _____ m

(c) between the market and the library
         _____ m

(d) between the market and the restaurant
         _____ m

(e) between the restaurant and the library
         _____ m

(f) Emma travelled from the market to the library, then to the playground. How far did she travel?
         _____ m

2 Holly, Hannah and Lulu each ran on the treadmill for 30 minutes.

Name	Distance
Holly	2.54 km
Ruby	3.05 km
Lulu	2.89 km

(a) What is the distance each girl ran?

Holly: ☐ m

Ruby: ☐ m

Lulu: ☐ m

(b) ☐ ran the greatest distance.

(c) ☐ ran the shortest distance.

(d) Arrange the girls according to the distance they ran, from the shortest to the greatest.

☐ , ☐ , ☐

Worksheet 11

Measuring Perimeters in Different Units

1 Measure and find the perimeter of each figure.

(a)

Perimeter = ☐ cm

= ☐ mm

(b)

Perimeter = ☐ cm

= ☐ mm

(c)

Perimeter = [   ] cm

= [   ] mm

(d)

Perimeter = [   ] cm

= [   ] mm

2 Find the perimeter of each figure in mm.

(a)

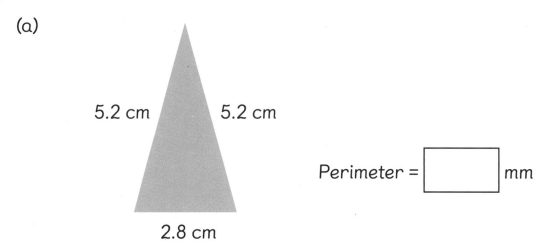

5.2 cm   5.2 cm

2.8 cm

Perimeter = ☐ mm

(b)

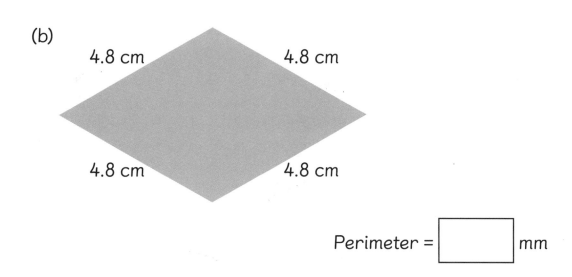

4.8 cm   4.8 cm

4.8 cm   4.8 cm

Perimeter = ☐ mm

(c)

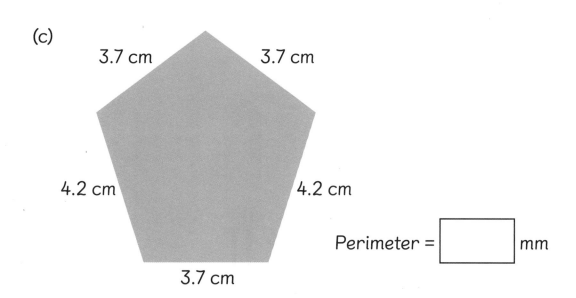

3.7 cm   3.7 cm

4.2 cm   4.2 cm

3.7 cm

Perimeter = ☐ mm

Worksheet 12

Solving Problems Involving Scale Reading

1 Read each measurement and fill in the blanks.

(a)

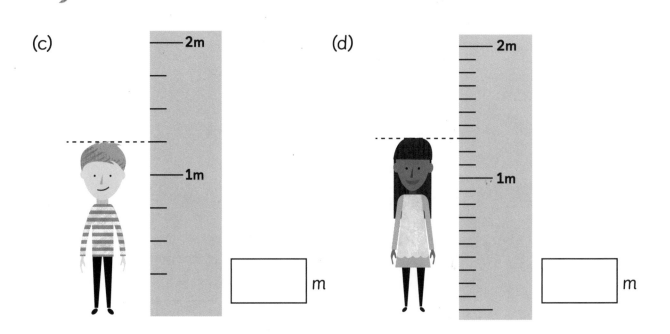

[____] m

(b)

[____] m

(c)

[____] m

(d)

[____] m

2 Read each measurement, or the total amount, and fill in the blanks.

(a)

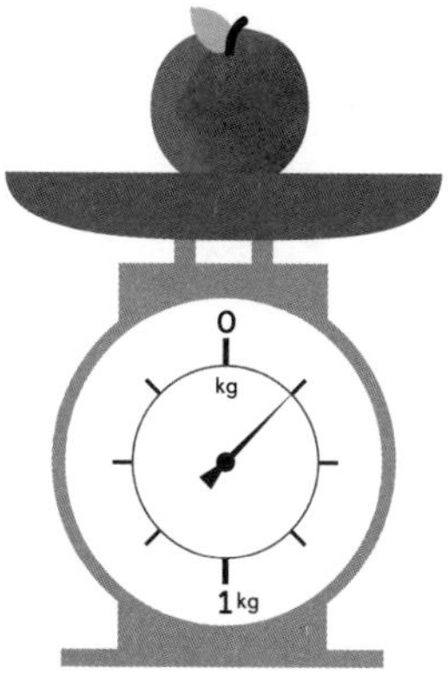

☐ kg

(b)

☐ kg

(c)

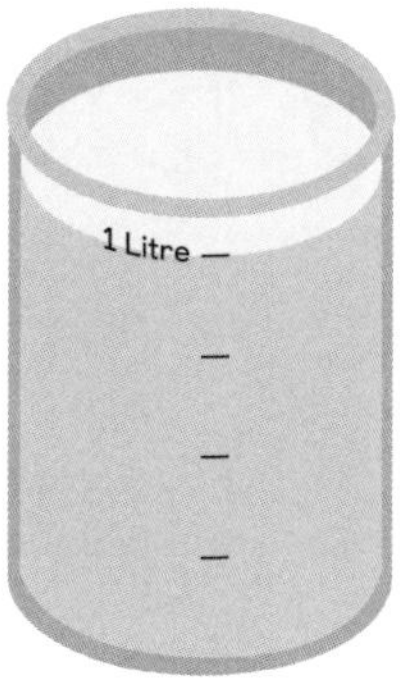

☐ l

(d)

☐ l

Date: _____

Hannah weighs two groups of multilink cubes and wood blocks. Each group gives the same scale reading.

Hannah wants to use only multilink cubes to get the same reading.
How many multilink cubes does she need?

Name: _____ Class: _____ Date: _____

Review 10

1 What is the mass of the bag of potatoes?

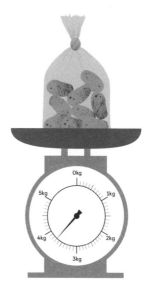

(a) Give the mass to the nearest 0.1 kg.  kg

(b) Give the mass to the nearest kg.   kg

2 Fill in the blanks.

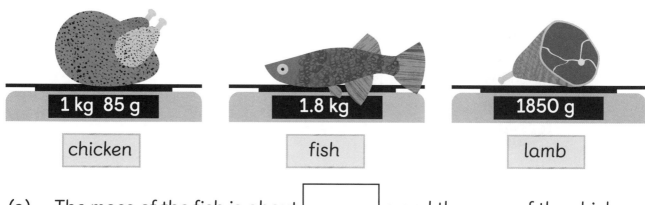

| 1 kg 85 g | 1.8 kg | 1850 g |
| chicken | fish | lamb |

(a) The mass of the fish is about [   ] g and the mass of the chicken

is about [   ] g.

(b) The [   ] is the lightest.

(c) The [   ] is the heaviest.

(d) The mass of the lamb is about [   ] kg, to the nearest kg.

3 Find the volume of the drinks in each container in ml.

(a)

1 Litre —

The volume of drink in the

container is about ⬚ ml.

(b)

Soda
0.45l

The volume of drink in the

container is about ⬚ ml.

(c)

Juice

3.3l

The volume of drink in the

container is about ⬚ ml.

4 Read the measurements and fill in the blanks.

(a)

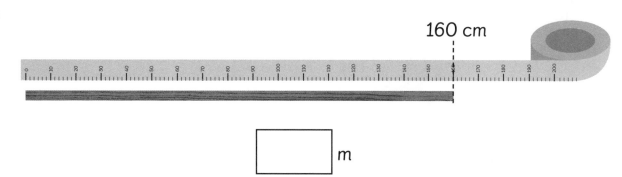

160 cm

[ ] m

(b)

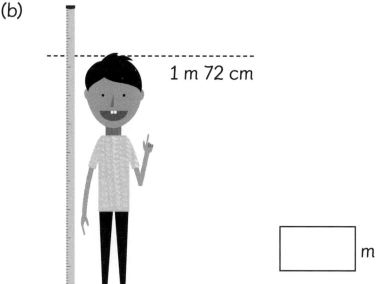

1 m 72 cm

[ ] m

5 Measure each side to the nearest cm and estimate its perimeter.

The perimeter of the figure is about [ ] cm.

6 Find the perimeter of each figure in mm.

(a)

3.5 cm   3.5 cm

3.5 cm

Perimeter = [   ] mm

(b)

6.9 cm

3.1 cm   3.1 cm

6.9 cm

Perimeter = [   ] mm

7 Convert the following.

(a)   0.99 km = [   ] m

(b)   1.36 km = [   ] m

(c)   2.7 km   = [   ] m

(d)   10.2 km = [   ] m

(e)   8.03 km = [   ] m

(f)   5.56 km = [   ] m

Revision 3

1 Fill in the place-value chart and then write the decimal.

(a)

0.1 0.1 0.1 0.1 0.1

0.01 0.01 0.01 0.01 0.01 0.01

Tenths	Hundredths

[ ] tenths + [ ] hundredths = [ ] + [ ]

= [ ]

(b)

1 1 1 1 0.01 0.01

Ones	Tenths	Hundredths

[ ] ones + [ ] tenths + [ ] hundredths

= [ ] + [ ] + [ ]

= [ ]

(c)

0.01 0.01 0.01 0.01 0.01 0.01

0.01 0.01 0.01 0.01 0.01 0.01

Tenths	Hundredths

[ ] hundredths = [ ] tenths + [ ] hundredths

= [ ] + [ ]

= [ ]

2 Fill in the blanks.

(a)

67.54

The digit [ ] is in the tenths place.

The digit [ ] is in the hundredths place.

The digit [ ] is in the tens place.

The digit [ ] is in the ones place.

(b)

13.89

The digit [ ] stands for 10.

The digit [ ] stands for $\frac{9}{100}$.

The digit [ ] stands for $\frac{4}{5}$.

3 Arrange the numbers in increasing order.

| 5.46 | 5.4 | 5.64 | 5.6 |

[ ] , [ ] , [ ] , [ ]

4 Write the length of the lolly as a fraction and as a decimal, then round it to the nearest cm.

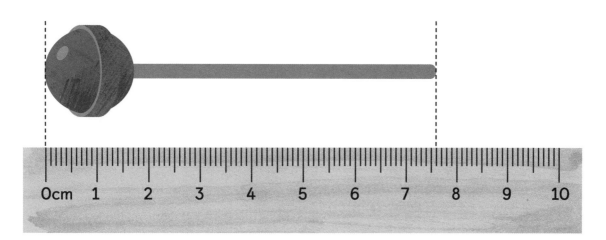

The length of the lolly is 7 $\dfrac{\boxed{}}{10}$ cm or $\boxed{}$ cm.

$\boxed{}$ cm ≈ $\boxed{}$ cm

5 Round the price of each item to the nearest £ and to the nearest £10.

(a)

£7.25 ≈ $\boxed{}$ (to the nearest £)

£7.25 ≈ $\boxed{}$ (to the nearest £10)

(b)

£30.89 ≈ $\boxed{}$ (to the nearest £)

£30.89 ≈ $\boxed{}$ (to the nearest £10)

(c)

£15.50 ≈ ⬚ (to the nearest £)

£15.50 ≈ ⬚ (to the nearest £10)

6 Fill in the blanks.

WOW

£1.35

£2.15

£0.99

£4.78

(a)  bought [pencil case] [pencil case] . Calculate the total cost.

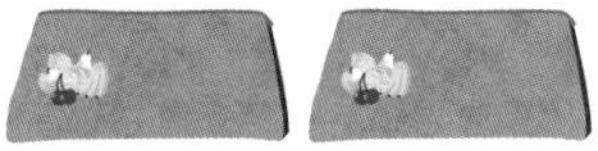

⬚

(b)  bought 5 [pens] . Calculate the total cost.

⬚

(c) ![girl] bought ![magazine] ![magazine] ![magazine] ![magazine] and she gave the cashier £10. Calculate the change.

[ ]

(d) ![boy] and ![girl] shared the cost of ![notebook] and ![magazine] equally. How much did each of them pay?

[ ]

(e) ![boy] and ![girl] shared the cost of ![notebook] ![notebook] ![notebook] ![notebook].

![boy] paid twice as much as ![girl]. How much did ![boy] pay?

[ ]

7 Fill in the blanks.

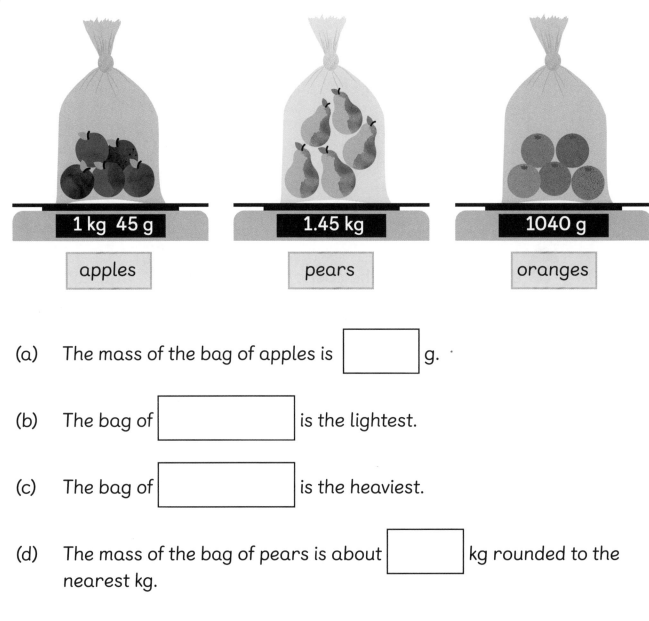

| 1 kg 45 g | 1.45 kg | 1040 g |
| apples | pears | oranges |

(a) The mass of the bag of apples is ☐ g.

(b) The bag of ☐ is the lightest.

(c) The bag of ☐ is the heaviest.

(d) The mass of the bag of pears is about ☐ kg rounded to the nearest kg.

(e) The total mass of the bags of apples, pears and oranges is ☐ g.

8 Fill in the blanks.

(a) 0.7 km = [   ] m

(b) 6.34 km = [   ] km [   ] m

(c) 37 cm = [   ] mm

(d) 5.62 m = [   ] m [   ] cm

(e) 2816 ml = [   ] l

(f) 7.42 l = [   ] l [   ] ml

9 Write each amount in £ and compare.

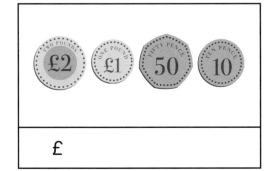

£ [   ]

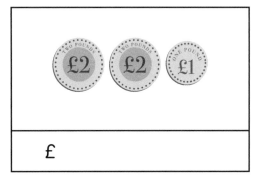

£ [   ]

£ [   ] is less than £ [   ].

10 Fill in the blanks. Write each answer as a decimal.

(a) $2 \div 10 =$ ⬚

(b) $16 \div 10 =$ ⬚

(c) $9 \div 100 =$ ⬚

(d) $48 \div 100 =$ ⬚

Area of Figures

Chapter 11

Name: _____ Class: _____ Date: _____

Worksheet 1

Measuring the Surface that an Object Covers

This is a 1-inch square tile.

1 Using the 1-inch square tile, estimate how much surface each figure covers.

(a)

This figure covers ☐ times the surface that the square tile covers.

(b)

This figure covers ☐ times the surface that the square tile covers.

(c)

This figure covers ☐ times the surface that the square tile covers.

(d)

This figure covers ☐ times the surface that the square tile covers.

(e)

This figure covers ☐ times the surface that the square tile covers.

Worksheet 2

Measuring Area

1 Arrange the figures into groups with the same number of tiles. Colour each group a different colour.

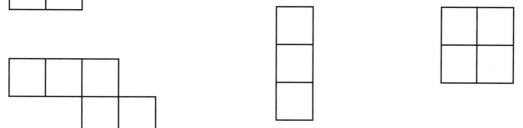

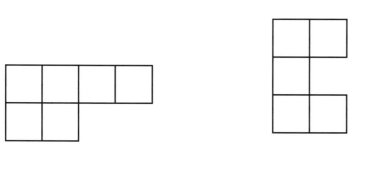

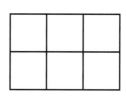

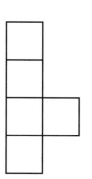

2 For each given figure, draw another figure with the same area.

(a)

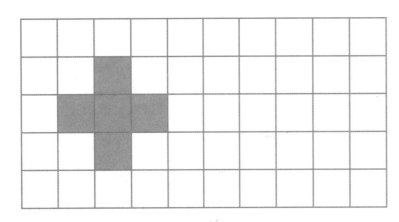

(b)

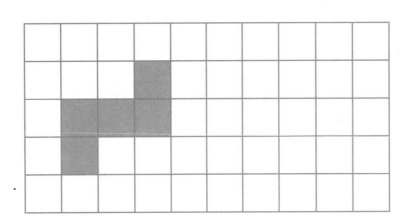

(c)

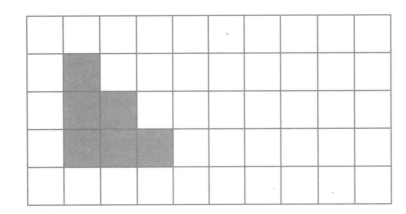

Name: _____ Class: _____ Date: _____

Worksheet 3

Measuring Area

1 Find the area of each figure, then find its perimeter.
Fill in the table below.

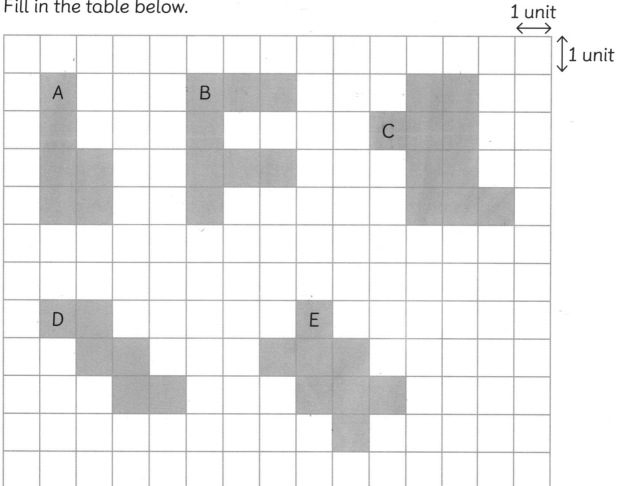

	Area	Perimeter
Figure A	square units	units
Figure B	square units	units
Figure C	square units	units
Figure D	square units	units
Figure E	square units	units

2 Draw two figures on the grid below that have both the same area and the same perimeter.

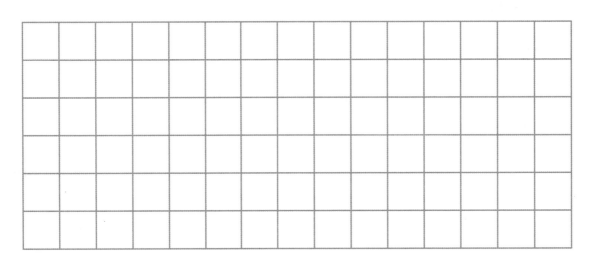

3 Draw two figures on the grid below which have the same area, but which have different perimeters.

Name: _____ Class: _____ Date: _____

Worksheet 4

Measuring Area

1 Find the area of each figure. Each ■ has an area of 1 square unit.

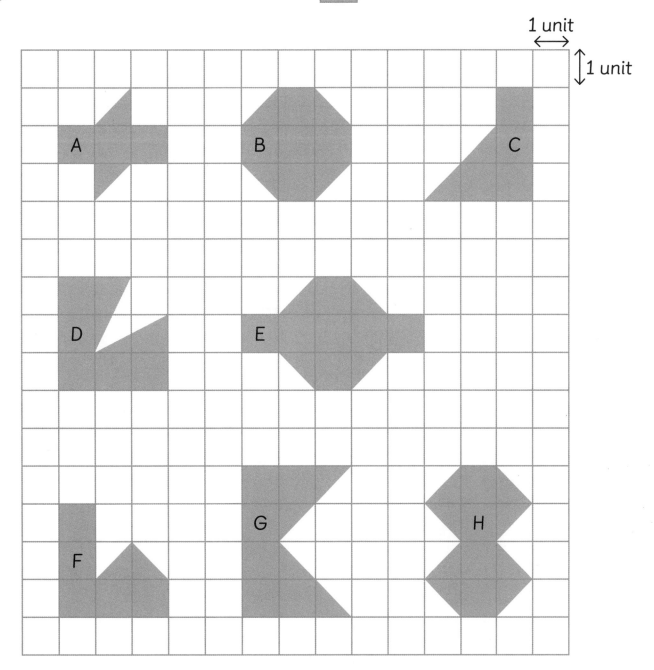

	Area
Figure A	square units
Figure B	square units
Figure C	square units
Figure D	square units
Figure E	square units
Figure F	square units
Figure G	square units
Figure H	square units

(b) Which figure has the largest area?

2 Shade more ⬜ or ◣ so that each figure has an area of 12 square units.

(a)

(b)

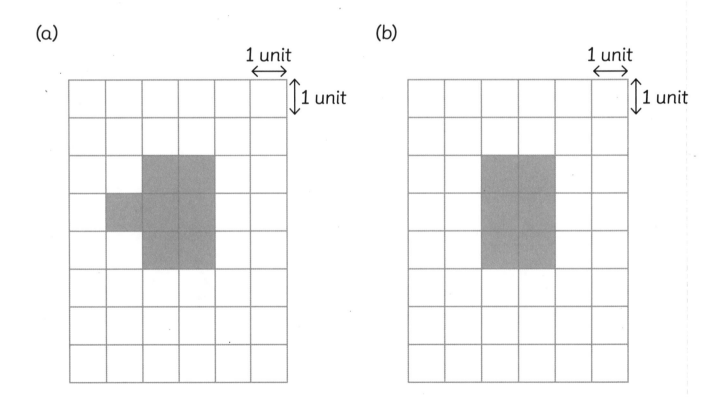

Worksheet 5

Measuring Area

1 Find the area of each rectangle using multiplication.

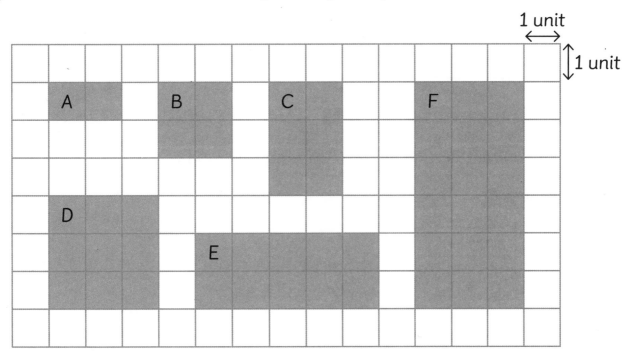

1 unit

1 unit

(a) [ ] × [ ] = [ ]

The area of figure A is [ ] square units.

(b) [ ] × [ ] = [ ]

The area of figure B is [ ] square units.

(c) [ ] × [ ] = [ ]

The area of figure C is [ ] square units.

(d)
$$\boxed{} \times \boxed{} = \boxed{}$$

The area of figure D is $\boxed{}$ square units.

(e)
$$\boxed{} \times \boxed{} = \boxed{}$$

The area of figure E is $\boxed{}$ square units.

(f)
$$\boxed{} \times \boxed{} = \boxed{}$$

The area of figure F is $\boxed{}$ square units.

2 Figure X is a rectangle with an area of 24 square units. It has 4 rows. Draw Figure X in the 1-unit square grid below.

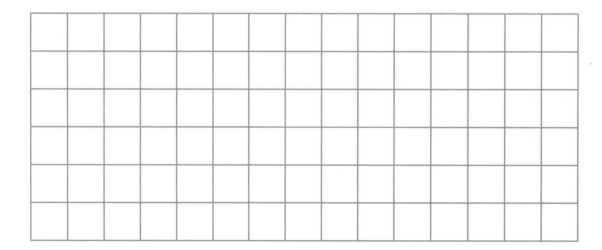

Worksheet 6

Measuring Area

1 Find the area of each figure.

(a)

Area of [ ] is 1 square unit.

Area of complete figure = [ ] square units.

(b)

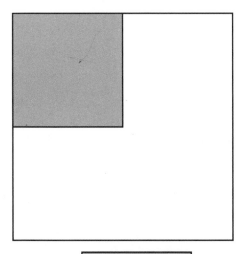

Area of [ ] is 1 square unit.

Area of complete figure = [ ] square units.

2 Find the area of each figure.

(a)

Area of 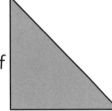 is 2 square units.

Area of complete figure = [ ] square units.

(b)

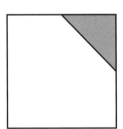

Area of is 1 square unit.

Area of complete figure = [ ] square units.

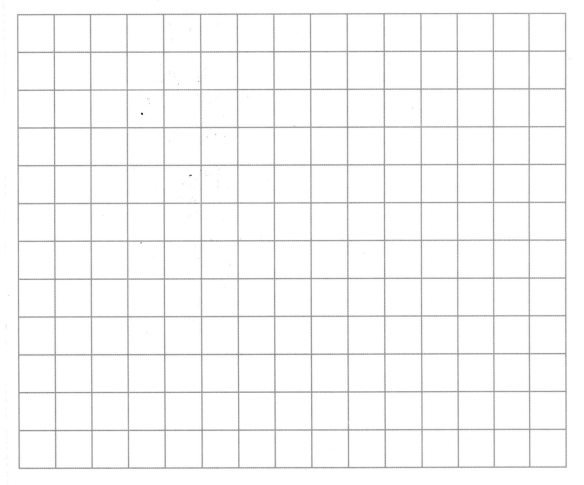

is 1 unit and the area of each ☐ is 1 square unit. Draw two figures on the grid below: both figures should have an area of 16 square units, but they should have different perimeters.

Among all possible figures on the grid having area 16 square units, what are the largest and the smallest possible perimeters?

Review 11

1 Find the area and the perimeter of each figure.
Fill in the table below.

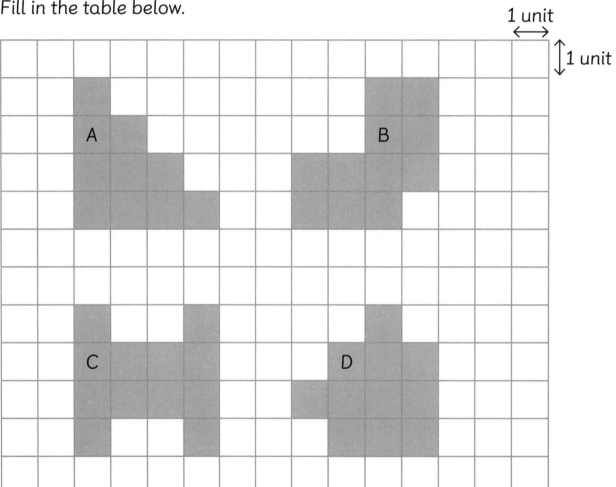

		Area	Perimeter
(a)	Figure A	square units	units
(b)	Figure B	square units	units
(c)	Figure C	square units	units
(d)	Figure D	square units	units

2 Find the area of each figure.
Fill in the table below.

1 unit ←→

1 unit ↕

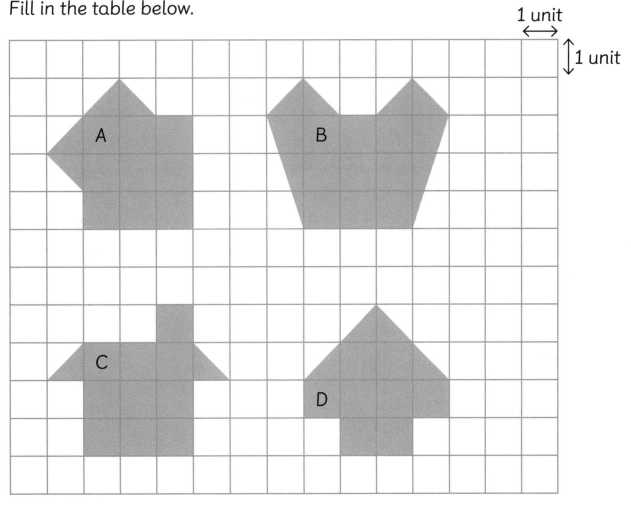

		Area
(a)	Figure A	square units
(b)	Figure B	square units
(c)	Figure C	square units
(d)	Figure D	square units

3 Find the area of each figure using multiplication.

(a)

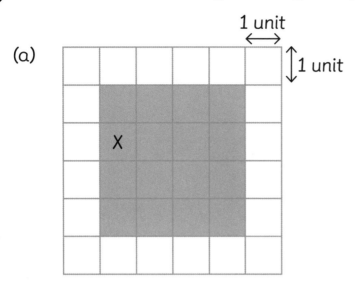

$$\boxed{} \times \boxed{} = \boxed{}$$

The area of figure X is $\boxed{}$ square units.

(b)

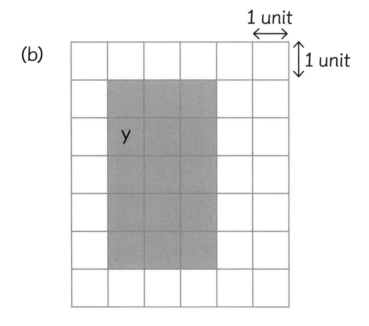

$$\boxed{} \times \boxed{} = \boxed{}$$

The area of figure Y is $\boxed{}$ square units.

4 Draw two figures on the grid paper that have the same perimeter but different areas.

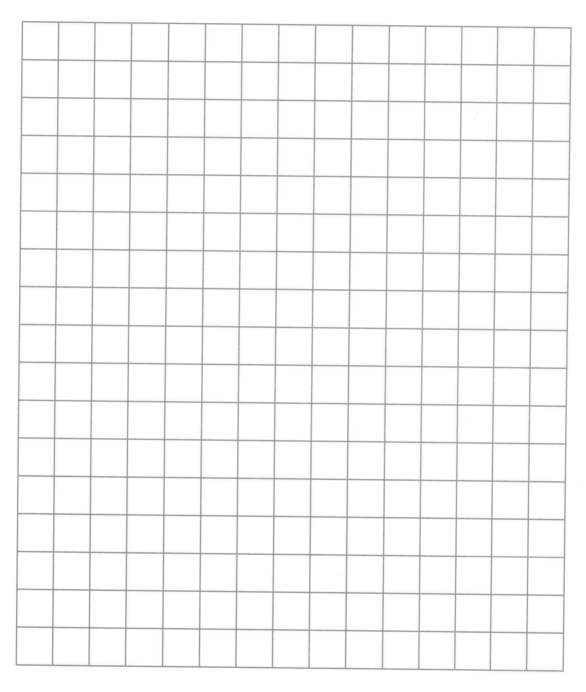

5 Draw two figures on the grid paper that have the same area but different perimeters.

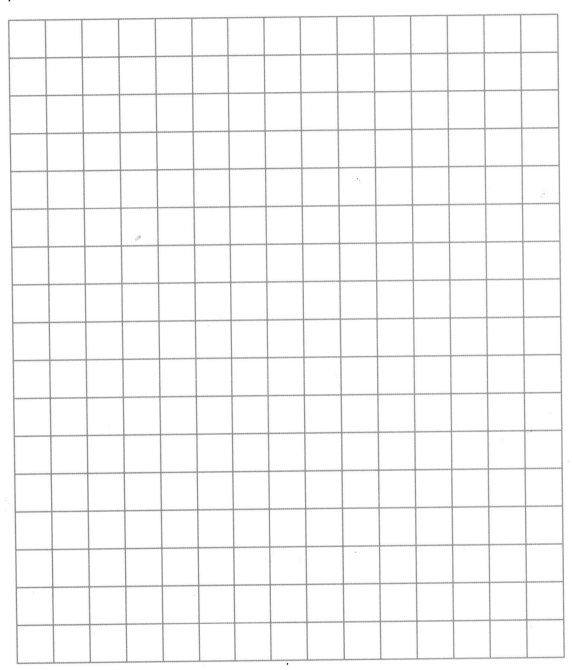

Geometry

Chapter 12

Name: _____   Class: _____   Date: _____

Worksheet 1

Knowing Types of Angles

1 Look at the angles in each of these figures.

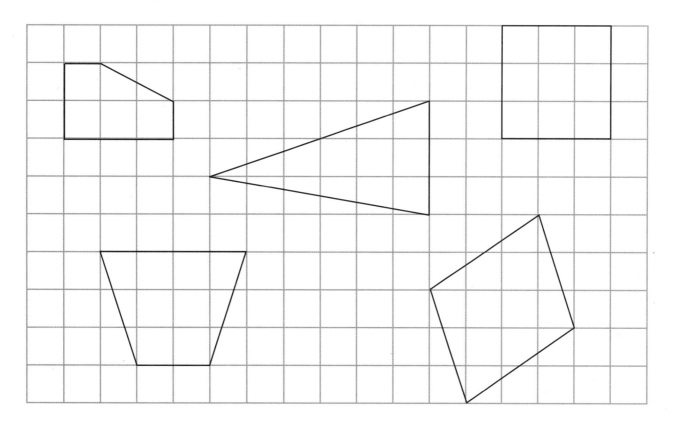

(a)   Colour all acute angles red.

(b)   Colour all right angles blue.

(c)   Colour all obtuse angles green.

2 Draw and label the following figures on the grid below.

    (a)   Figure A with 3 acute angles

    (b)   Figure B with 4 right angles

    (c)   Figure C with 1 acute angle, 1 obtuse angle and 2 right angles

    (d)   Figure D with 1 obtuse angle and 2 acute angles

Worksheet 2

Comparing Angles

1 Circle the largest angle in each figure.

(a)

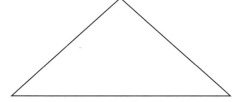

(b)

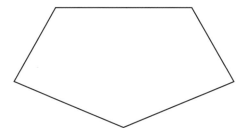

(c)

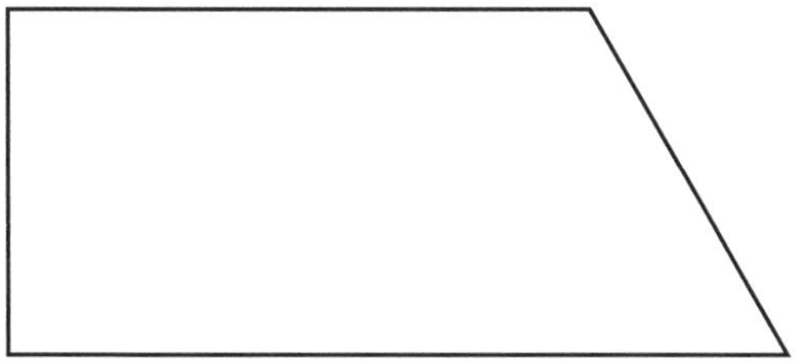

(d)

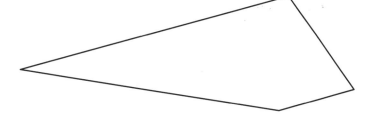

(e)

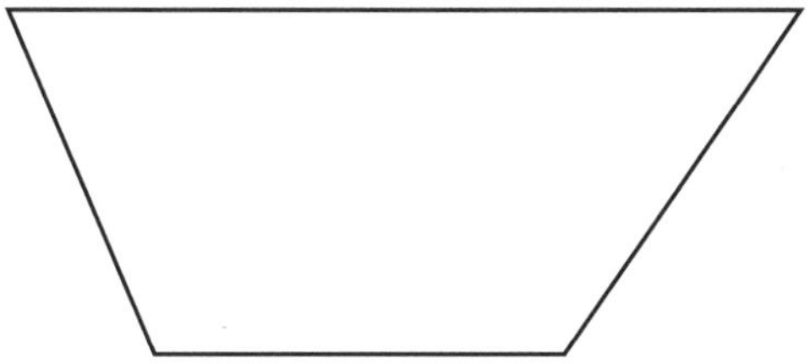

2 Which angle is smaller?

(a)

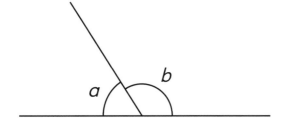

Angle _____ is smaller than angle _____ .

(b)

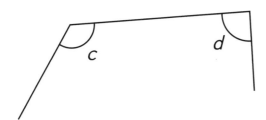

Angle _____ is smaller than angle _____ .

3 Which angle is the smallest?

(a)

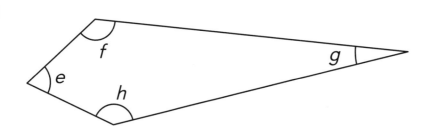

Angle _____

(b)

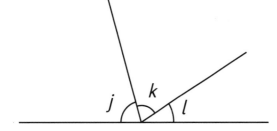

Angle _____

4 Arrange each group of angles from the largest to the smallest.

(a)

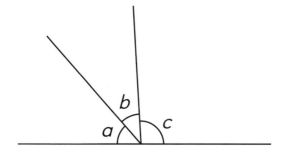

angle [ ] , angle [ ] , angle [ ]

(b)

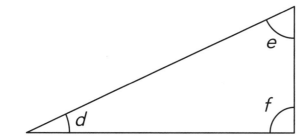

angle [ ] , angle [ ] , angle [ ]

(c)

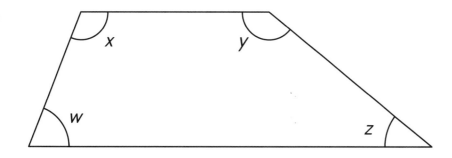

angle [ ] , angle [ ] , angle [ ] , angle [ ]

Name: _____ Class: _____ Date: _____

Worksheet 3

Classifying Triangles

1 Look at the triangles.

    (a)   Colour the scalene triangles green.

    (b)   Colour the equilateral triangles red.

    (c)   Colour the other isosceles triangles blue.

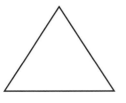 Label each triangle.

(a)

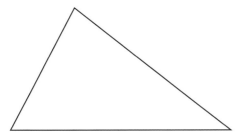

(b)

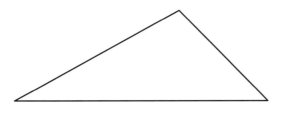

(c)

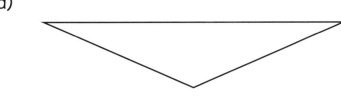

(d)

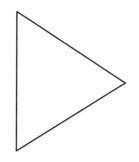

(e)

3 Draw two different scalene triangles.

4 Draw two different equilateral triangles.

5 Draw two different isosceles triangles.

Name: _____ Class: _____ Date: _____

Worksheet 4

Classifying Quadrilaterals

1 Look at the quadrilaterals given.

(a) Colour the squares blue.
(b) Colour any other rectangles green.
(c) Colour the other rhombuses red.
(d) Colour any other parallelograms yellow.
(e) Colour any other trapeziums orange.

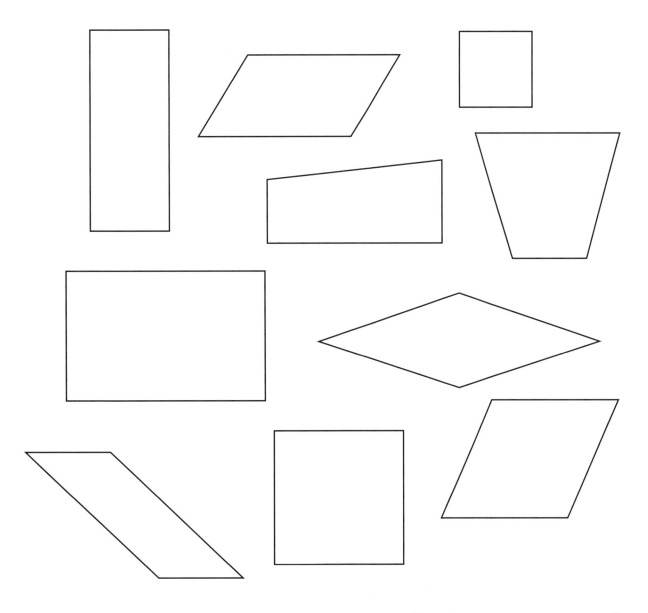

2 Label each quadrilateral.

(a)

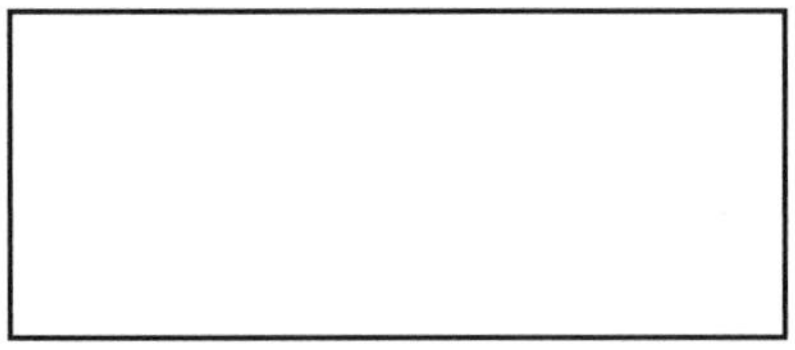

[ ]

(b)

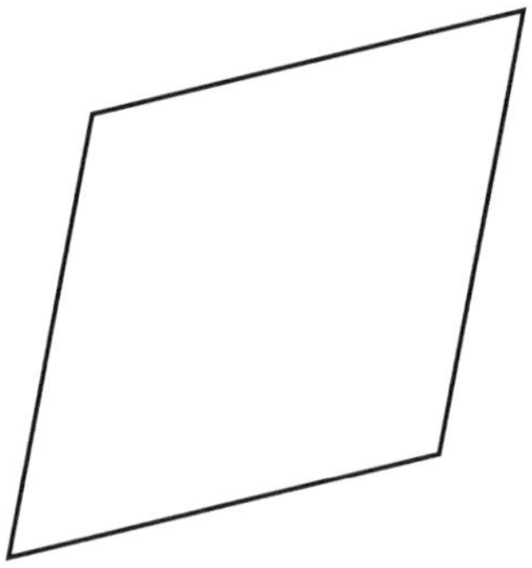

[ ]

(c)

[ ]

(d)

[ ]

(e)

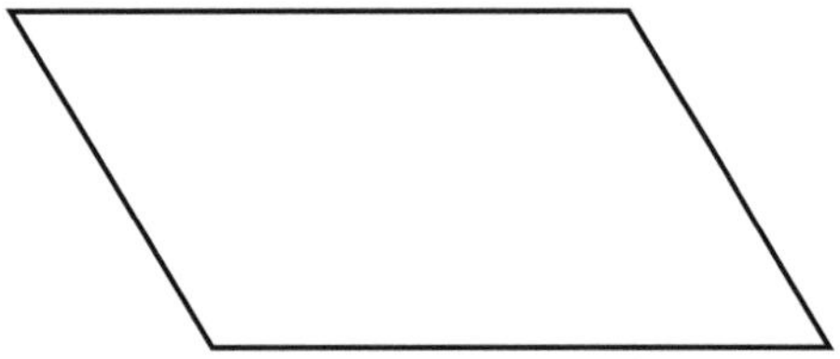

[ ]

3 Draw and label the following quadrilaterals on the grid.

(a)   Draw a square and label it A.

(b)   Draw a rectangle and label it B.

(c)   Draw a rhombus and label it C.

(d)   Draw a parallelogram and label it D.

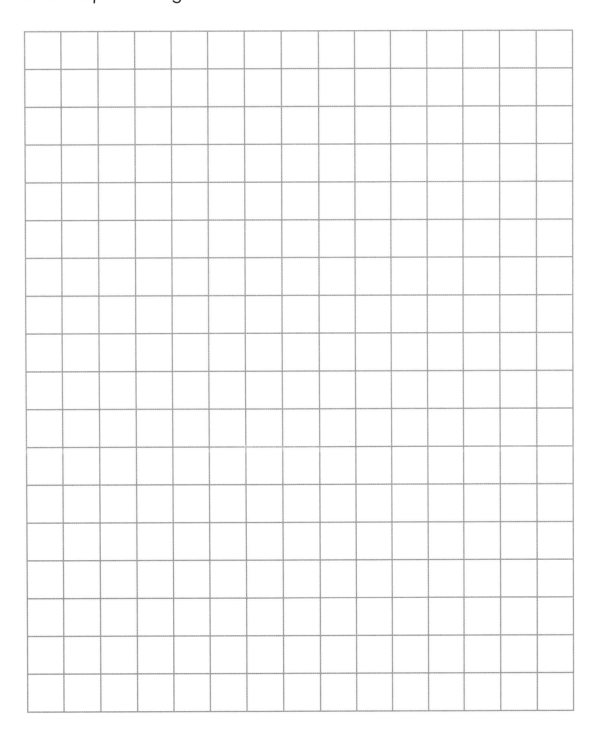

4 Draw 5 different trapeziums on the grid below.

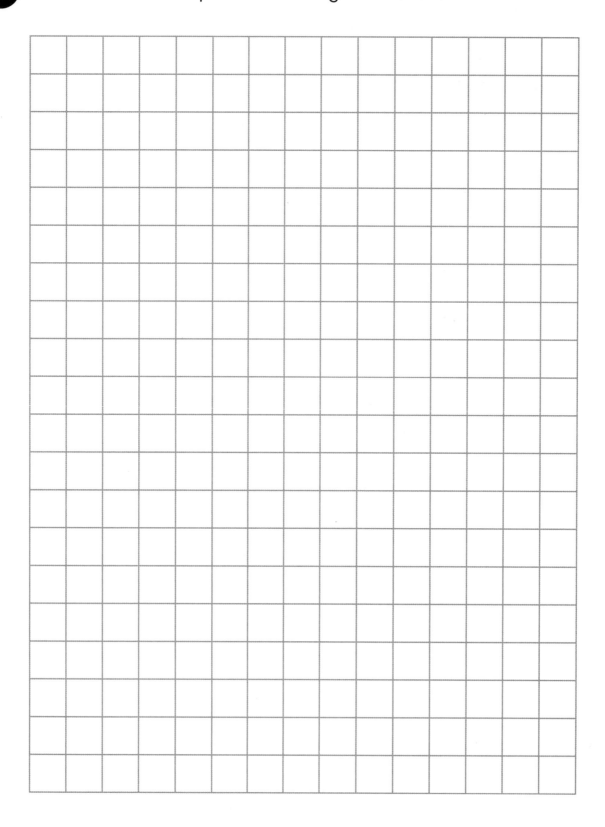

Worksheet 5

Identifying Symmetrical Figures

1 Circle the symmetric figures.

(a)

(b)

(c)

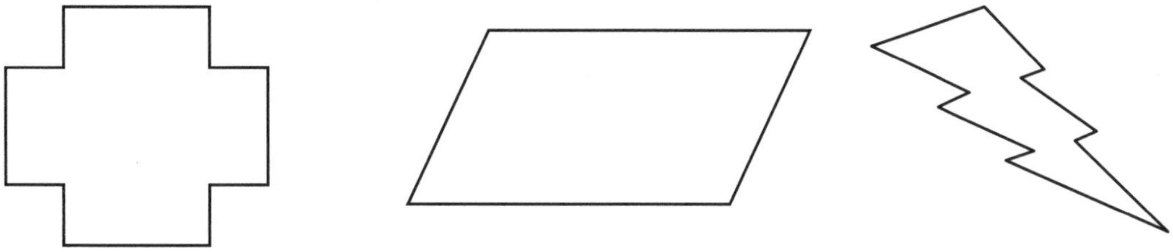

(d)

Worksheet 6

Drawing Lines of Symmetry

1 Draw the line of symmetry in each figure.

(a)

(b)

(c)

(d)

2 Draw one line of symmetry in each figure.

(a)

(b)

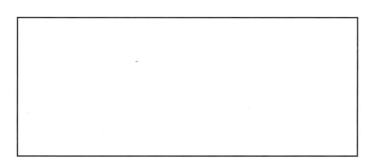

(c)

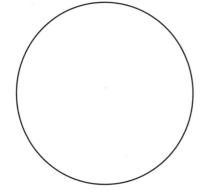

(d)

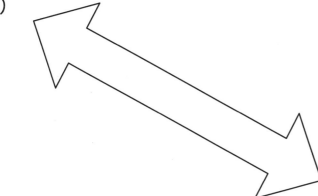

Draw all the lines of symmetry in each figure.

(a)

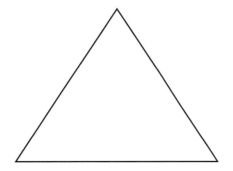

(b)

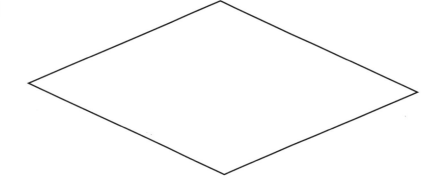

(c)

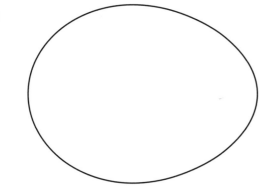

(d)

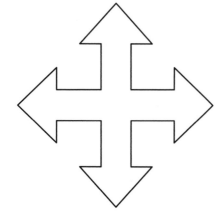

4 Use the letters below to fill in the blanks.

MATHEMATICS

(a) Which letters are symmetrical?

(b) Which letters have only one line of symmetry?

(c) Which letters have two lines of symmetry?

(d) Which letter does not have a line of symmetry?

5 Think about all the letters in the alphabet.
Which letters can have more than two lines of symmetry?

Worksheet 7

Completing Symmetrical Figures

1 Each dotted line represents a line of symmetry of the completed figure. Complete each figure.

(a)

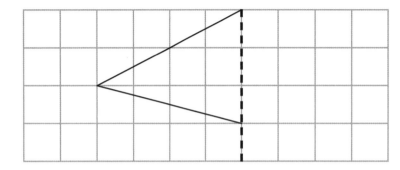

(b)

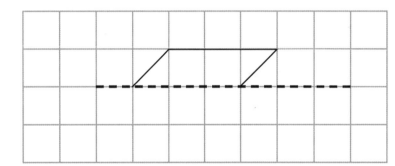

(c)

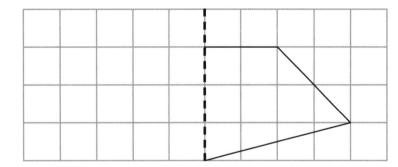

(d)

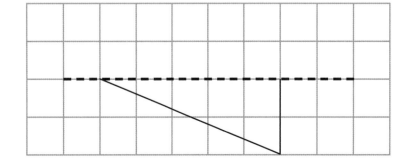

2 The dotted lines are lines of symmetry.
Complete each figure.

(a)

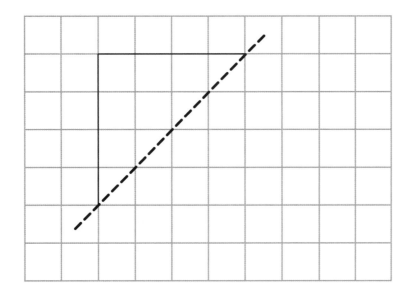

(b)

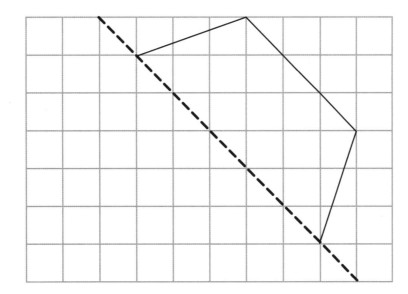

3 Complete each figure to make the dotted line a line of symmetry.

(a)

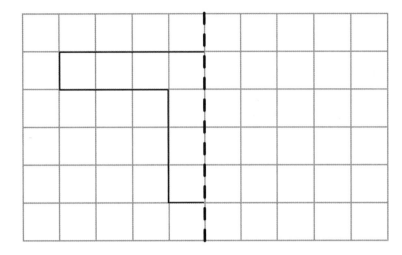

(b)

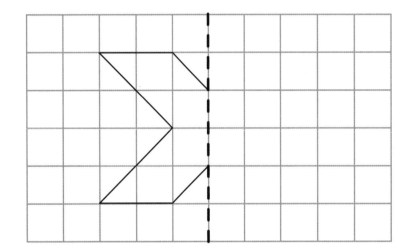

(c)

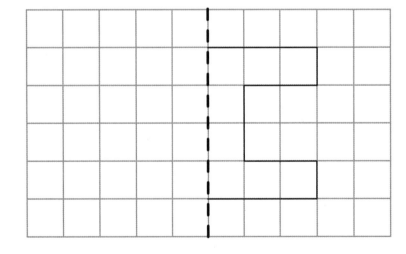

Worksheet 8

Making Symmetrical Figures

1   puts two drops of paint on each sheet of paper.

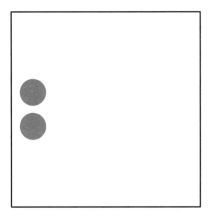

The diagrams below show some sheets of paper after they are unfolded.
Draw the line of symmetry to show how each sheet was folded.

(a)

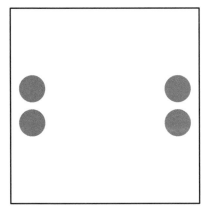

(b)

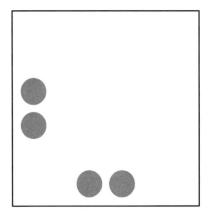

(c)

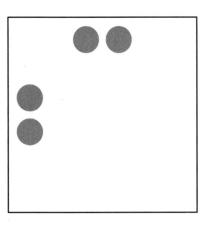

(d)

2 paints a rectangle on the four sheets of paper shown on the left. She then folds each sheet along a line of symmetry. Complete the diagrams on the right to show how each sheet of paper looks after it is folded and then opened up.

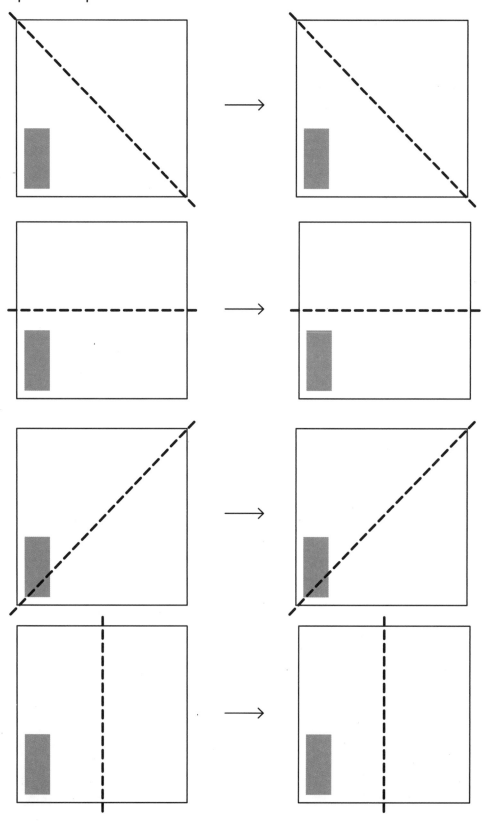

Worksheet 9

Completing Symmetrical Figures

1 Complete each pattern.

(a)

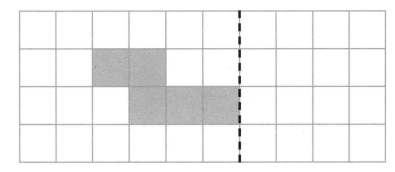

(b)

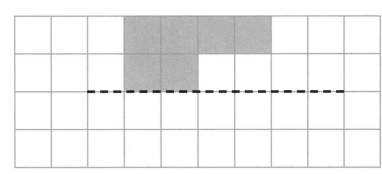

(c)

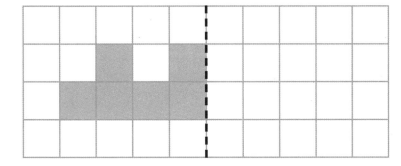

(d)

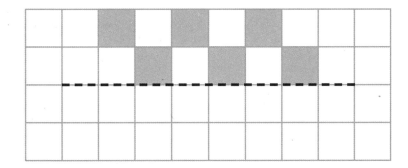

2 Complete each figure so that it is symmetrical about the dotted line.

(a)

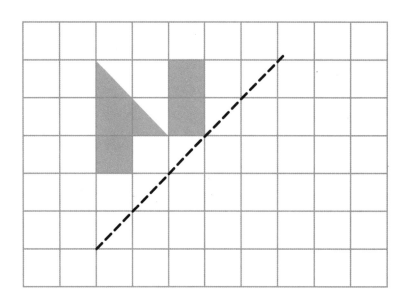

(b)

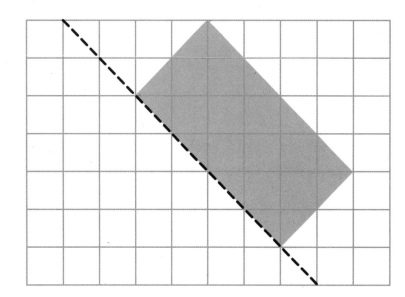

Name: _____ Class: _____ Date: _____

Sorting Shapes

 drew some polygons.

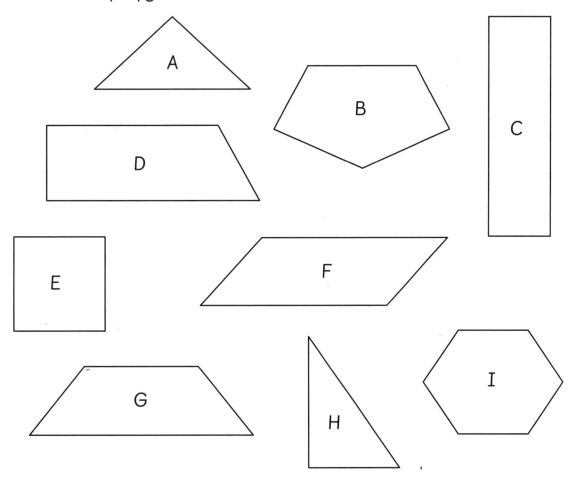

Look at the polygons and fill in the blanks.

1 Which figures have no line of symmetry?

2 Which figures have more than one line of symmetry?

3 Classify the polygons A–I and complete each table.

(a)

3 sides	4 sides	more than 4 sides

(b)

no parallel sides	has 1 pair of parallel sides	has more than 1 pair of parallel sides

(c)

has at least a right angle	no right angle

(d)

no obtuse angle	has at least 1 obtuse angle

Use 5 ▨ to form 10 different symmetric figures.

Draw each figure in the grid below.

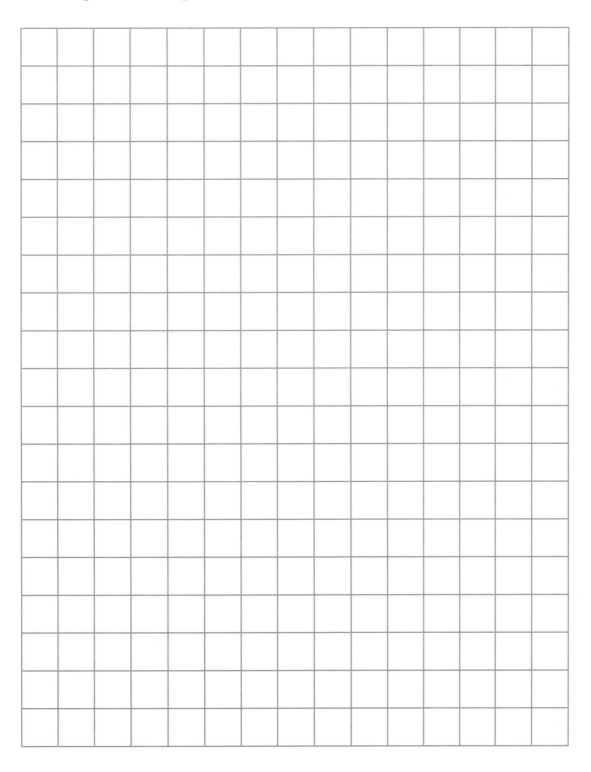

Name: _____ Class: _____ Date: _____

Review 12

1 Arrange each group of angles from the smallest to the largest.

(a)

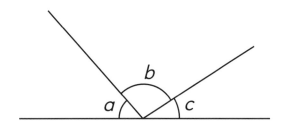

angle ⬚ , angle ⬚ , angle ⬚

(b)

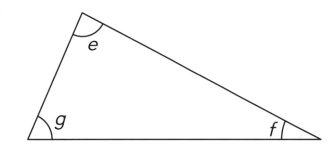

angle ⬚ , angle ⬚ , angle ⬚

2 Draw the line of symmetry in each figure.

(a)

(b)

3 Complete each figure so that it is symmetrical about the dotted line.

(a)

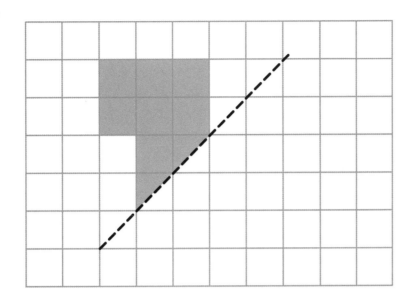

(b)

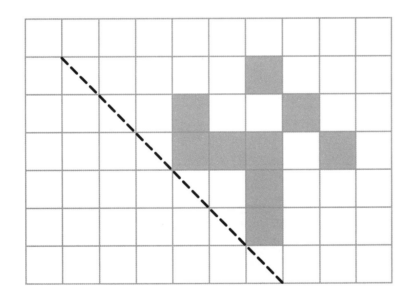

4 Classify the polygons and complete each table.

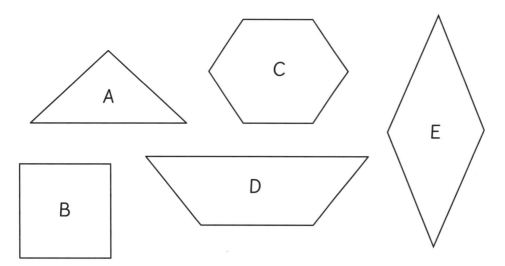

(a)

no acute angles	has at least 1 acute angle

(b)

no parallel sides	has 1 pair of parallel sides	has more than 1 pair of parallel sides

Position and Movement

Chapter 13

Name: _____ Class: _____ Date: _____

Worksheet 1

Describing Position

1 , , and 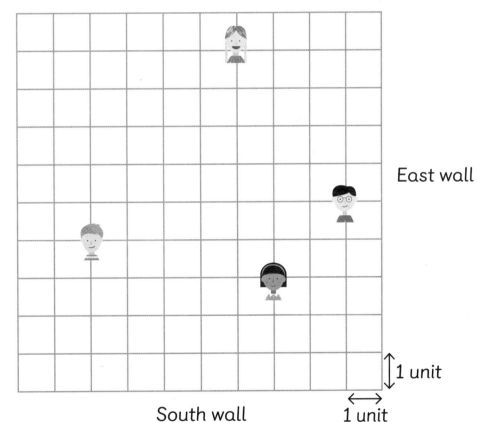 are standing at different locations in the hall.

Describe their positions.

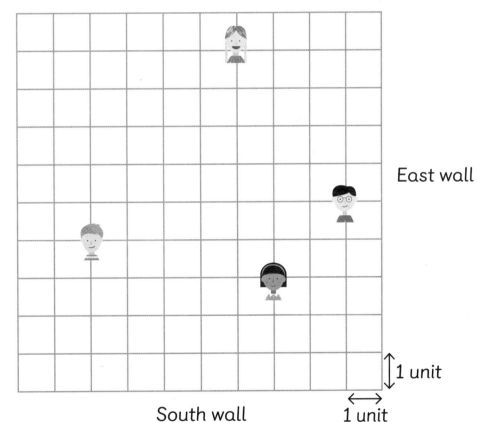

North wall

West wall   East wall

South wall   1 unit   1 unit

(a) 👓 is

☐ units from the North wall.

☐ units from the East wall.

☐ units from the South wall.

☐ units from the West wall.

(b) 🙂 is

☐ units from the North wall.

☐ units from the East wall.

☐ units from the South wall.

☐ units from the West wall.

(c) 🙂 is

☐ units from the North wall.

☐ units from the East wall.

☐ units from the South wall.

☐ units from the West wall.

(d) ![face] is

[   ] units from the North wall.

[   ] units from the East wall.

[   ] units from the South wall.

[   ] units from the West wall.

2 Describe the positions of the vertices of Rectangle ABCD.

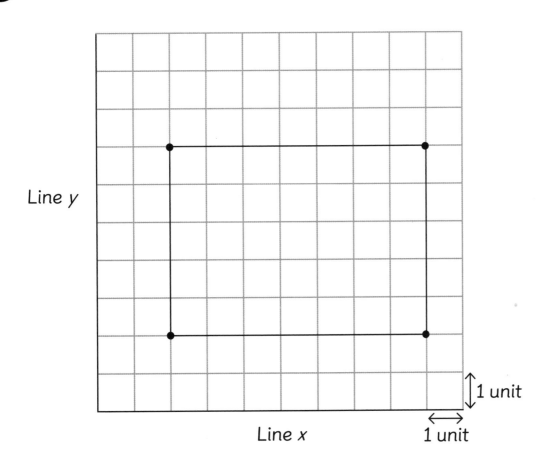

Line *y*

Line *x*

1 unit

1 unit

(a)   Point A:

| | units from Line y
| | units from Line x

(b)   Point B:

| | units from Line y
| | units from Line x

(c)   Point C:

| | units from Line y
| | units from Line x

(d)   Point D:

| | units from Line y
| | units from Line x

Name: _____ Class: _____ Date: _____

Describing Position

1 Describe the positions of the points using coordinates.

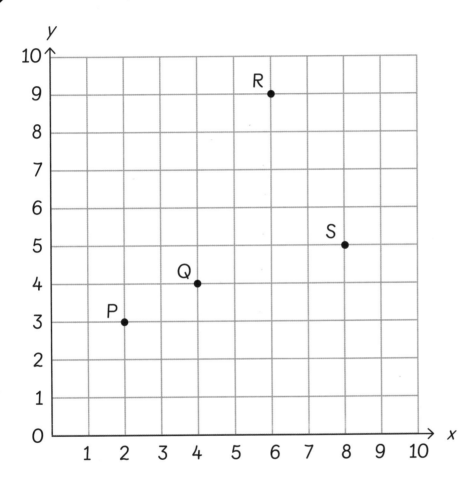

(a)   Point P is ⬜ units from the y-axis.

Point P is ⬜ units from the x-axis.

Point P is at (⬜ , ⬜).

(b)   Point Q is ☐ units from the *y*-axis.

Point Q is ☐ units from the *x*-axis.

Point Q is at (☐ , ☐) .

(c)   Point R is ☐ units from the *y*-axis.

Point R is ☐ units from the *x*-axis.

Point R is at (☐ , ☐) .

(d)   Point S is ☐ units from the *y*-axis.

Point S is ☐ units from the *x*-axis.

Point S is at (☐ , ☐) .

2 A, B, C and D are the vertices of a quadrilateral. Describe the positions of the vertices using coordinates.

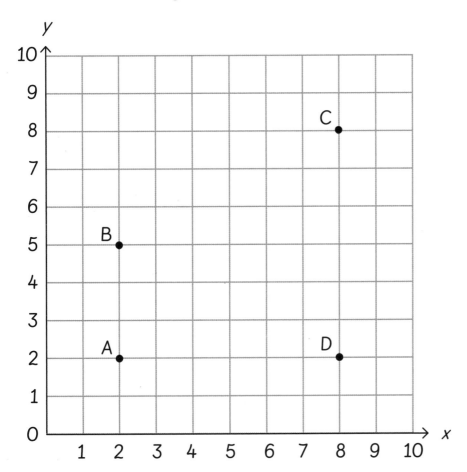

(a)   Point A is ☐ units from the y-axis.

Point A is ☐ units from the x-axis.

Point A is at (☐ , ☐).

(b)   Point B is ☐ units from the y-axis.

Point B is ☐ units from the x-axis.

Point B is at (☐ , ☐).

(c)   Point C is [ ] units from the *y*-axis.

Point C is [ ] units from the *x*-axis.

Point C is at ([ ] , [ ]) .

(d)   Point D is [ ] units from the *y*-axis.

Point D is [ ] units from the *x*-axis.

Point D is at ([ ] , [ ]) .

(e)   What kind of quadrilateral is ABCD?   [   ]

3 Plot the other two vertices of square EFGH and name all the vertices using coordinates.

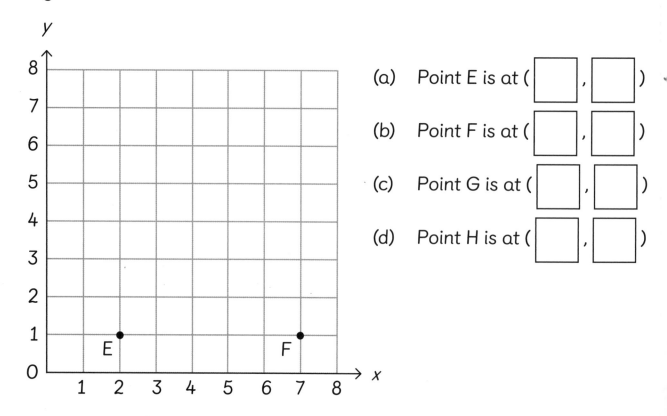

(a)   Point E is at ([ ] , [ ])

(b)   Point F is at ([ ] , [ ])

(c)   Point G is at ([ ] , [ ])

(d)   Point H is at ([ ] , [ ])

Worksheet 3

Plotting Points

1 Plot the vertices of each figure given on the next page, and name the shape.

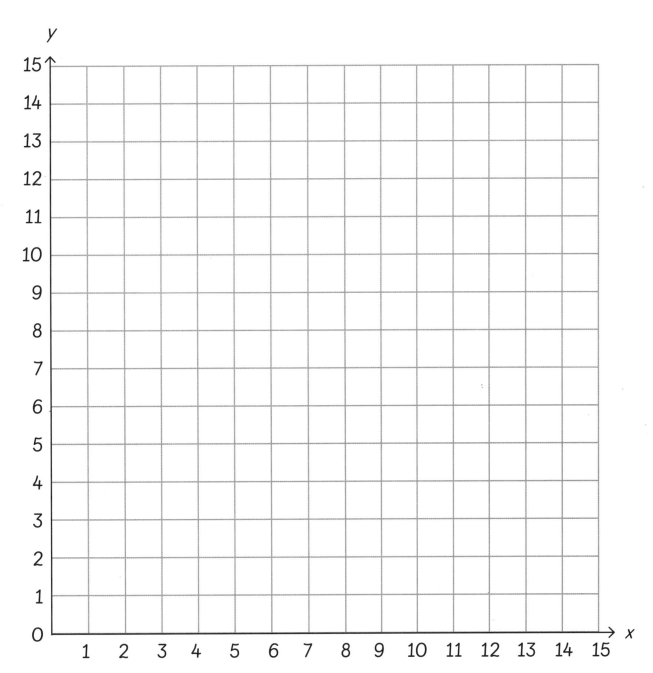

(a) Figure ABC

A (1,1), B (5,1), C (4,5)

Figure ABC is a [   ] .

(b) Figure DEFG

D (2,10), E (11,10), F (11,7), G (2,7)

Figure DEFG is a [   ] .

(c) Figure HIJK

H (3,15), I (5,15), J (8,11), K(3,11)

Figure HIJK is a [   ] .

(d) Figure LMNO

L (10,15), M (14,14), N (11,11), O (14,10)

Figure LMNO is a [   ] .

(e) Figure PQRS

P (6,3), Q (10,5), R (14,3), S (10,1)

Figure PQRS is a [   ] .

Worksheet 4

Describing Movements

1 Some points are drawn on a square grid.

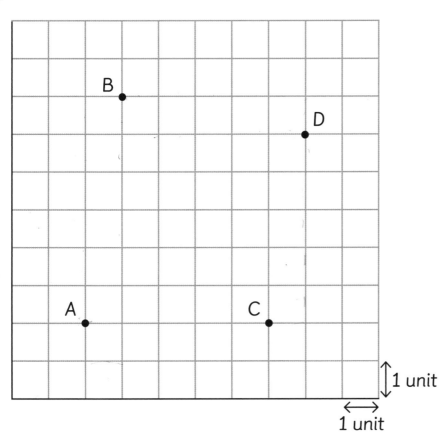

Describe these movements

(a) From Point A to Point B:

A translates [   ] unit to the right then [   ] units upwards.

(b) From Point B to Point C:

[   ]

(c)   From Point D to Point A:

(d)   From Point D to Point B:

(e)   Point A translates 4 units to the right and 5 units upwards to Point P.
        Plot Point P on the grid.

2 Show where 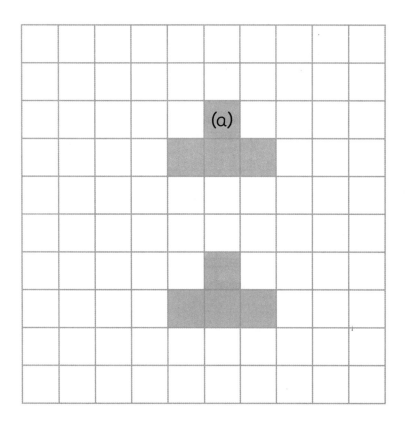 ends up at the end of each translation.

The first translation is done for you.

(a)

(a) moves up by 4 units.

(b) moves down by 2 units.

(c) moves to the left by 4 units.

(d) moves to the right by 3 units.

(e) moves to the right by 2 units and then moves up by 6 units.

Worksheet 5

Describing Movements

1 A parallelogram is drawn on a square grid.

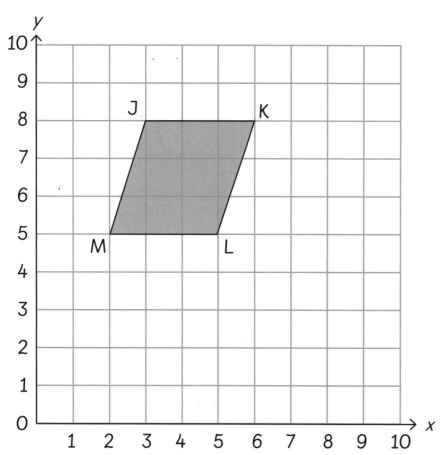

Describe the translation of parallelogram JKLM that results in:

(a) Point J moving to (4,7):

(b) Point K moving to (10,4):

(c)   Point L moving to (10,0):

(d)   Point M moving to (5,2):

2 A triangle is drawn on a square grid.

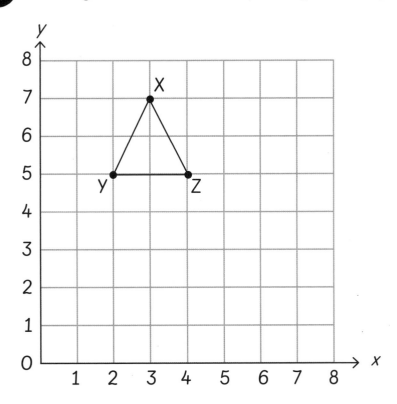

Describe two different translations which move the triangle XYZ so that one of its vertices ends up at (6,3).

(a)

(b)

Date: _____

Draw a parallelogram EFGH on the square grid having the same area as the trapezium ABCD.

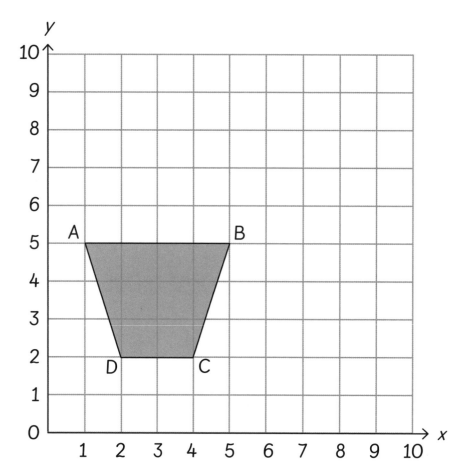

Review 13

1 Plot the points and describe the shape formed by each set of coordinates.

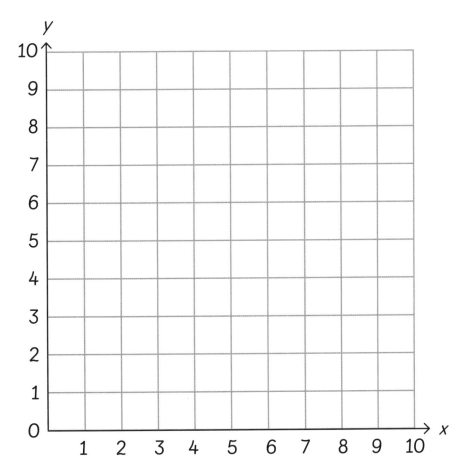

(a)   Figure ABC

A (3,6), B (4,9), C (5,6)

Figure ABC is a [   ].

(b)   Figure DEFG

D (6,6), E (8,10), F (10,10), G (8,6)

Figure DEFG is a [   ].

(c)   Figure HIJK

      H (2,0), I (0,4), J (6,4), K (6,0)

      Figure HIJK is a [   ] .

2 Describe the translations taking **A** to each of the positions B, C, D.

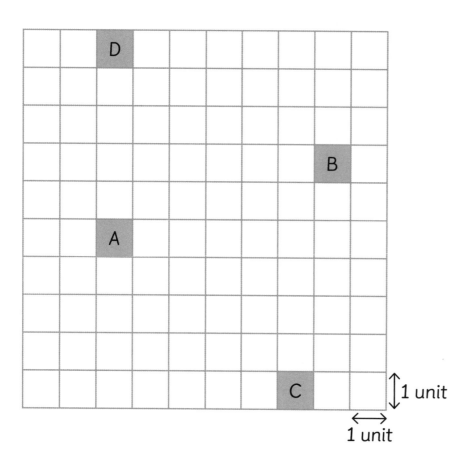

1 unit

1 unit

(a)   From A to B:

[   ]

(b)   From A to C:

[   ]

(c)   From A to D:

<table>
<tr><td></td></tr>
</table>

3 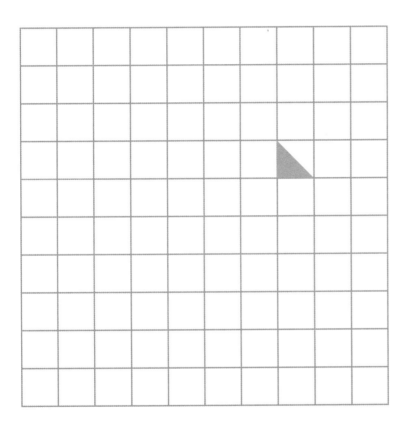 translates 7 units to the left and then 6 units downwards.

Draw to show the new position of 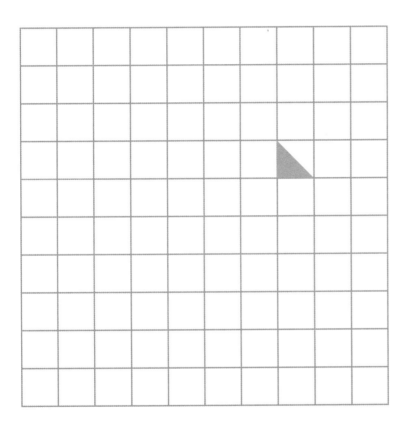 on the grid.

4 WXYZ is a parallelogram. The vertices W, X and Y are given by:

W (1, 1)   X (3, 6)   Y (10, 6)

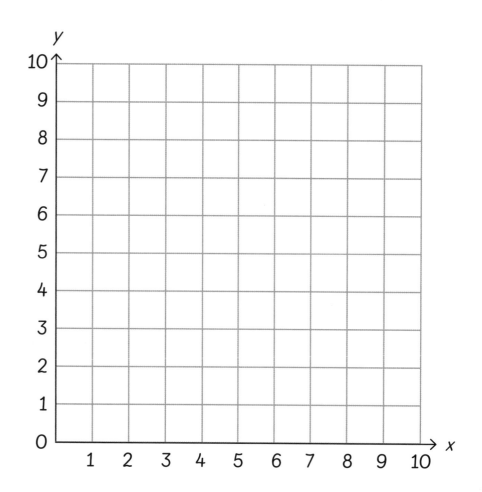

Plot the vertices W, X, Y and name the coordinates of Z.

Z is at [   ].

Roman Numerals

Chapter 14

Name: _____ Class: _____ Date: _____

Worksheet 1

Writing Roman Numerals for 1 to 20

1 Help Holly find her way home.
Write the Roman numerals next to the numbers given.

1

2

3

4

5

6

7

8

9

10

11

12

13

14

15

16

17

18

19

20

V •

IV •

XIII •

VIII •

XV •

VI •

XIX •

• 13

• 8

• 5

• 15

• 4

• 3

• 6

• 19

Worksheet 2

Writing Roman Numerals to 100

1 Write the Roman numerals next to the numbers given.

5			55	
10			60	
15			65	
20			70	
25			75	
30			80	
35			85	
40			90	
45			95	
50			100	

2 Match.

LVII ●	● 21
XXI ●	● 74
LXXIV ●	● 57
XXXI ●	● 39
XVIII ●	● 99
LXXV ●	● 48
XCIX ●	● 31
XLVIII ●	● 75
	● 18

3 Complete the table.

Numbers	Roman Numerals
16	
	XXIV
33	
40	
	LI
	LXVI
69	
	LXXV
77	
96	

Date:_____

In Roman numerals:

I	stands for	1
V	stands for	5
X	stands for	10
L	stands for	50
C	stands for	100

Charles is looking for numbers from 1 to 100 that use more than 5 letters when written in Roman numerals. One such number is given. Find ten more such numbers, and the Roman numeral of each one. Are there others?

Numbers	Roman Numerals
28	XXVIII

Review 14

1 The age of each person in a family is shown.
Write each age in Roman numerals next to the numbers given.

5

11

16

18

21

42

47

73

2 Write the number represented by each Roman numeral.

II Summer
Olympic Games
Paris

II	

XI Winter
Olympic Games
Sapporo

XI	

XVI Summer
Olympic Games
Melbourne

XVI	

XII Summer
Olympic Games
Helsinki

XII	

VI Winter
Olympic Games
Oslo

VI	

XXIV Summer
Olympic Games
Seoul

XXIV	

XIX Winter
Olympic Games
Salt Lake City

XIX	

XXIX Summer
Olympic Games
Beijing

XXIX	

Name: _____ Class: _____ Date: _____

Revision 4

1 Find the area and the perimeter of each figure.

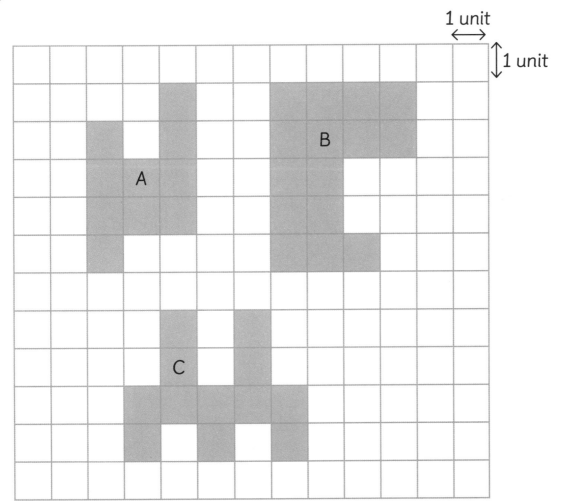

1 unit

1 unit

		Area	Perimeter
(a)	Figure A	square units	units
(b)	Figure B	square units	units
(c)	Figure C	square units	units

2 Figures D and E are drawn on 1-unit square grids. Find the area of each figure.

(a)

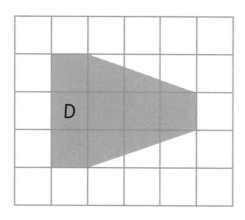

Area of Figure D

= [　　　] square units

(b)

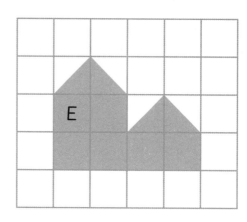

Area of Figure E

= [　　　] square units

3 Find the area of each figure using multiplication.

1 unit ⟷

⇕ 1 unit

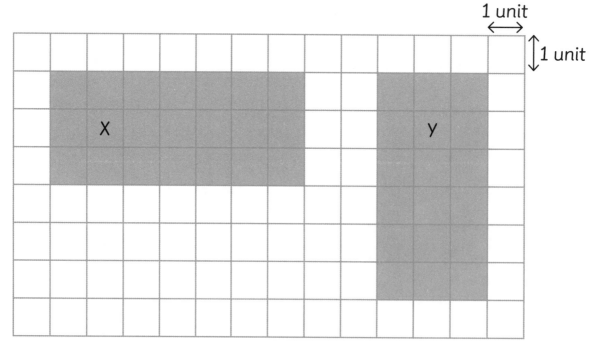

(a)　Area of X = [　　　] square units

(b)　Area of Y = [　　　] square units

4 Choose from the letters below to fill in the blanks.

MATHS NO PROBLEM

(a) Which letters have only one line of symmetry?

| |
| |

(b) Which letters have more than one line of symmetry?

| |
| |

(c) Which letters have no lines of symmetry?

| |
| |

5 Complete each figure to make a shape that is symmetrical about the dotted line.

(a)

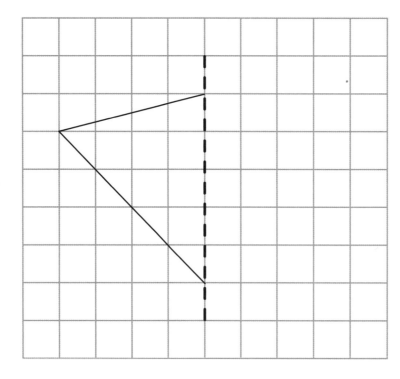

(b)

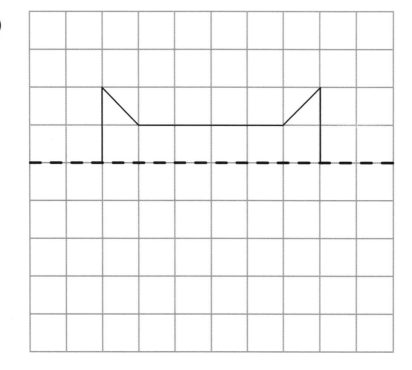

(c)

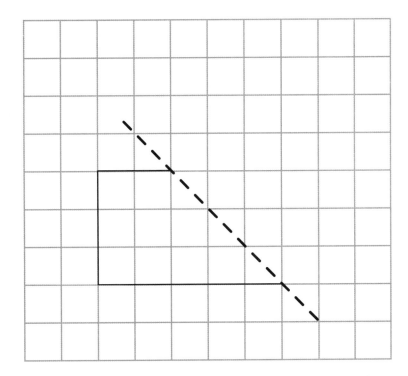

(d)

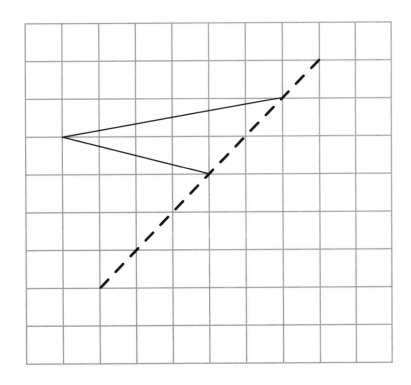

6 Classify the polygons A – F into three different groups and complete each table.

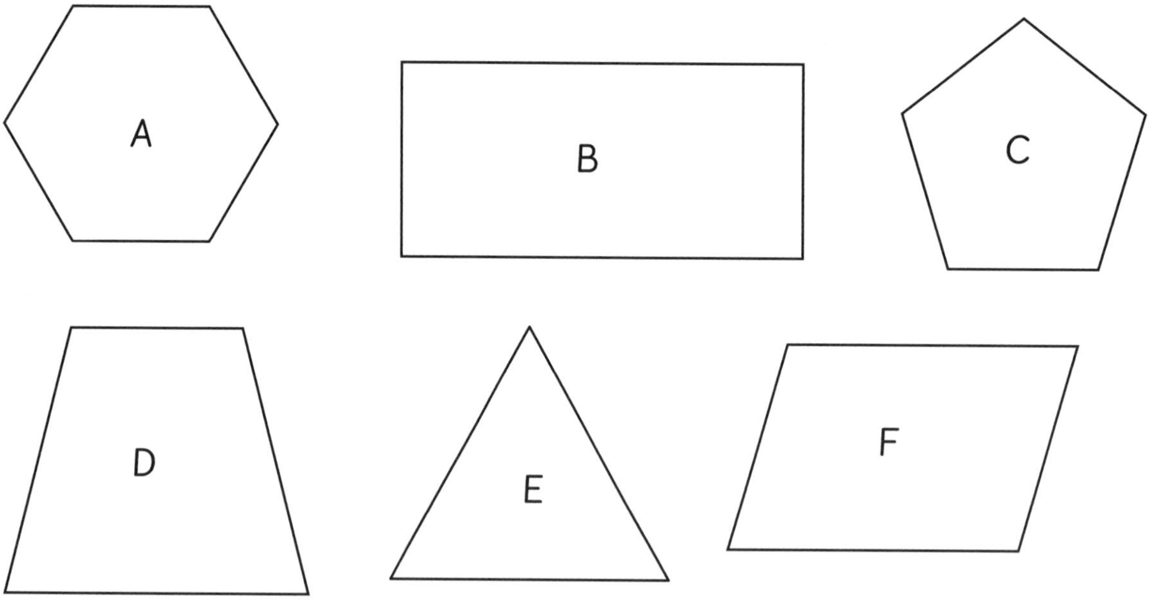

A

B

C

D

E

F

(a)

(b)

(c)

7 Describe each translation.

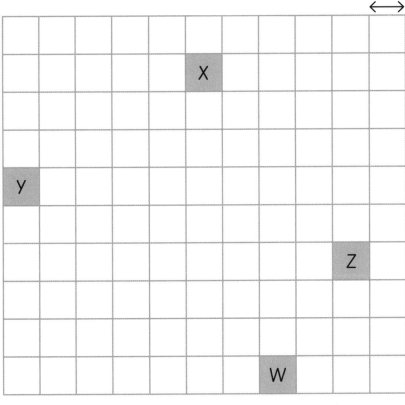

1 unit

1 unit

(a) From X to Y:

(b) From W to Z:

(c) From Y to W:

(d) From Y to X:

(e) From Z to Y:

8 Shade to show the new position of 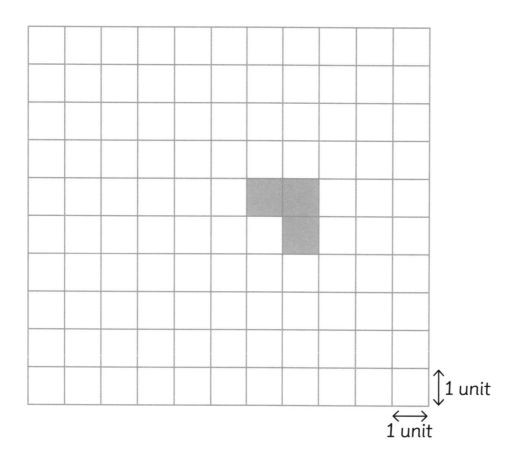 after each translation.

Start from the original position each time.

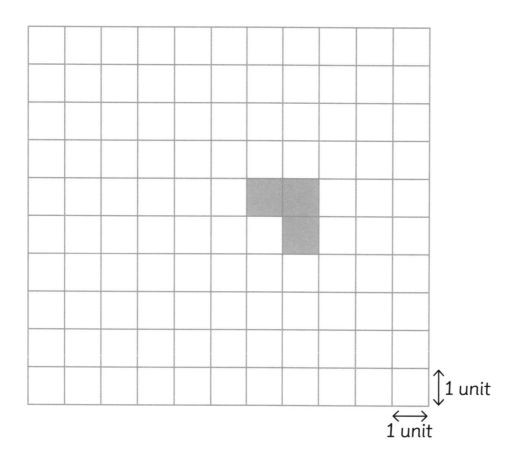

1 unit

1 unit

(a) translates 3 units upwards.

(b) translates 4 units downwards.

(c) translates 5 units to the left.

(d) translates 2 units to the right.

9 Fill in the blanks.

Numbers	Roman Numerals
4	
	XII
16	
18	
	XXII
	XXIX
35	
	XXXVIII
39	
	XLIV
46	
	LII
60	
	LXXXVII
95	

10 Arrange the angles from the largest to the smallest.

(a)

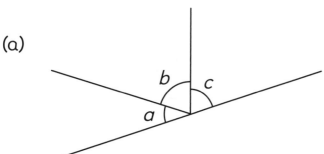

angle ⬚ , angle ⬚ , angle ⬚

(b)

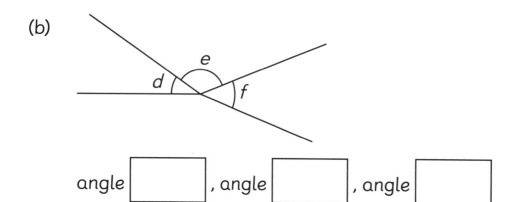

angle ⬚ , angle ⬚ , angle ⬚

(c)

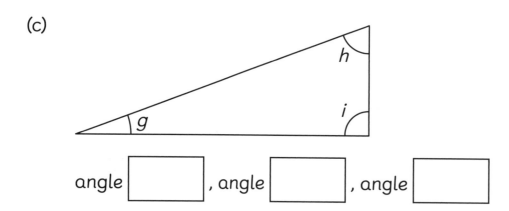

angle ⬚ , angle ⬚ , angle ⬚

(d)

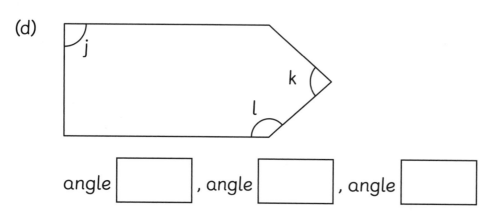

angle ⬚ , angle ⬚ , angle ⬚

End-of-Year Revision

Section A
Choose the correct answer.
Write the correct answer – (1), (2), (3) or (4) – in the brackets to the right.

1 What is 900 + 70 + 9 + 5000?

(1)   5799

(2)   5979

(3)   9579

(4)   9795

(   )

2 In the number 61.52, what is the value of the digit 2?

(1)   2 ones

(2)   2 tenths

(3)   20 tenths

(4)   2 hundredths

(   )

3 What is the sum of 64 hundredths and 25 tenths?

(1)   3.14

(2)   31.4

(3)   8.9

(4)   89

(   )

4 What is the total amount of water in the three beakers?

    (1)   25 l

    (2)   2.5 l

    (3)   2.05 l

    (4)   0.25 l

        (   )

5 What is the mass of the potatoes rounded to the nearest kg?

6kg 500g

    (1)   6 kg

    (2)   6.5 kg

    (3)   7 kg

    (4)   7.5 kg

        (   )

6 Write $\frac{2}{5}$ as a decimal.

(1) 0.2

(2) 0.4

(3) 0.5

(4) 0.02

(   )

7 Which of these words has only one letter with no line of symmetry?

(1) GEOMETRY

(2) NUMBER

(3) VOLUME

(4) FRACTION

(   )

8 Which angle is the smallest?

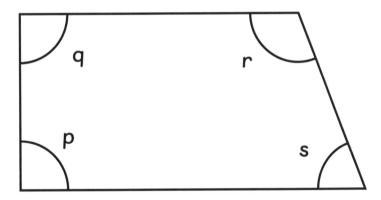

(1) p

(2) q

(3) r

(4) s

(   )

9 Find the value of 216 ÷ 6.

    (1)   21

    (2)   36

    (3)   41

    (4)   46

(   )

10 K translates 4 units to the right and 4 units downwards. What is the new position of K?

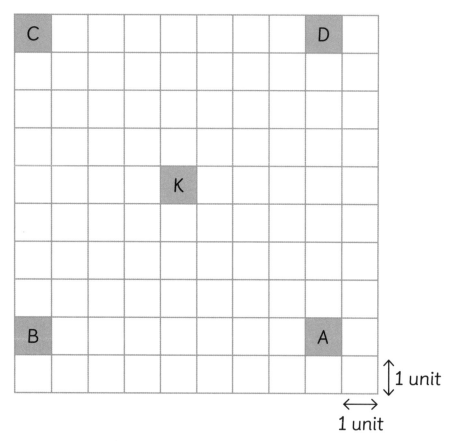

    (1)   A

    (2)   B

    (3)   C

    (4)   D

(   )

Section B

Write your answers in the spaces provided.

11 Write 9908 in words.

12 Arrange the decimals in increasing order.

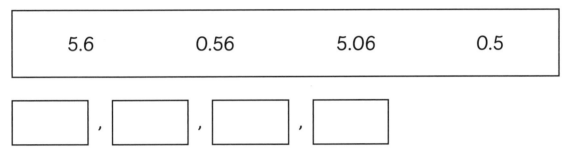

	,		,		,	

13 Write the number represented by the Roman numeral CXVII.

14 Round 4545 to the nearest 1000.

15 Multiply.

$$
\begin{array}{r}
4 \quad 9 \quad 2 \\
\times \qquad 7 \\
\hline
\end{array}
$$

16 What is the missing fraction?

$$\frac{2}{7} + \boxed{\quad ? \quad} = 1$$

17 's violin lesson is 1 h 20 min long.

It started at 11:45. At what time did her lesson end?

Give your answer using the 24-hour clock.

18 What is the missing Roman numeral on the watch?

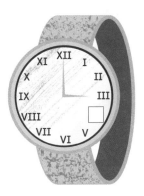

(answer box)

19 Write the amount of money in £.

£ (answer box)

20 What is the remainder when 110 is divided by 7?

(answer box)

21 Divide and give the answer as a decimal.

$15 \div 100 =$ [?]

22 87.63 is 0.01 more than [?]. What is the missing decimal?

23 $3\frac{1}{4} - \frac{3}{4} =$ [?]

Subtract and give your answer as a mixed number in its simplest form.

24 Add and give your answer as a mixed number.

$$\frac{4}{7} + \frac{4}{7} = \boxed{\quad ? \quad}$$

25 Complete the figure so that it is symmetrical about the dotted line.

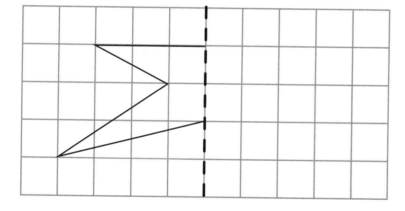

26 Each ☐ has an area of 1 square unit. Find the area of the figure.

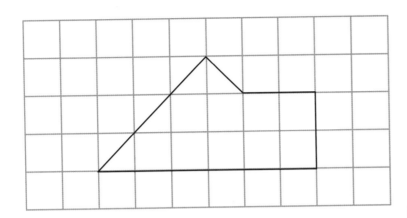

☐ square units

27 25 min 50 s = ☐ ? ☐ s

What is the missing number?

☐

28 What is the missing mixed number?

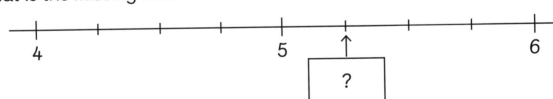

☐

29 Show $1\dfrac{2}{6}$, $1\dfrac{2}{3}$, $2\dfrac{10}{12}$ and 2.5 on the number line.

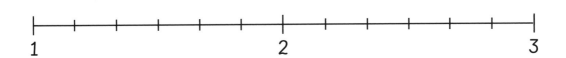

30 Measure the sides of the triangle and find the perimeter in mm?

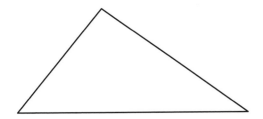

  mm

31 Lulu and 7 of her friends shared 594 stickers equally.

How many stickers were left over?

32 Holly and Amira have a total of 96 beads.

Holly has 5 times as many beads as Amira has.

How many beads does Holly have?

33 A fridge and a television cost a total of £2937.

The television costs £1299. What is the difference between the price of the fridge and the price of the television?

34 How many cupfuls of water are there altogether?

Give your answer as a mixed number in the simplest form.

35 These are the operating hours of a clinic on a weekday. How long is the clinic open on each weekday?

Grace Clinic

08:30 to 11:45
14:00 to 17:00

36 Sam has 50 red marbles.

He has 16 more red than green marbles.

He packed all of them into mixed bags of 7 marbles each.

How many bags did he pack?

Use the square grid to answer questions 37 to 40.

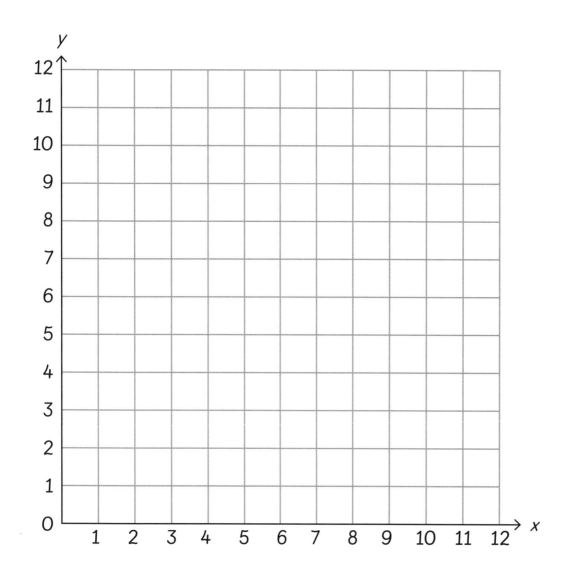

37 Plot and label points A,B and C on the square grid.

Point A (5, 9)

Point B (2, 6)

Point C (5, 3)

38 If quadrilateral ABCD is a rhombus, what are the coordinates of point D?

39 If point D is at (11, 9), what kind of quadrilateral is ABCD?

40 Find the coordinates of point D such that ABCD has just one line of symmetry.

Section C

Solve the word problem.

Show your work clearly.

41 Hannah had £37.80 to go shopping.

She spent twice as much money as she had left at the end.

How much did she spend?

42 There are 170 people in a hall.

There are 6 times as many girls as boys.

There are 6 more boys than teachers.

How many teachers are there?

43 The graph shows the number of pears a shop sold each day in a particular week.

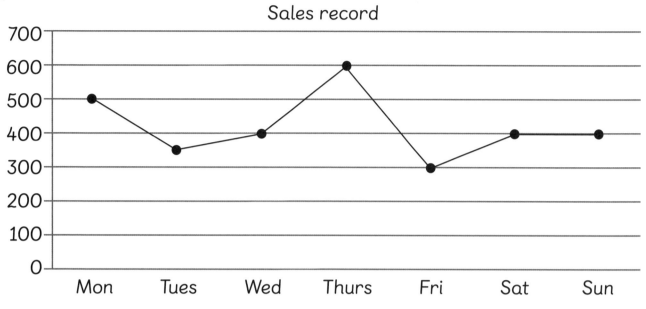

(a) On which two days were the same number of pears sold?

and

(b) On which day were twice as many pears sold as were sold on Friday?

(c) What was the greatest increase in the number of pears sold from one day to the next?

(d) The pears were sold at 5 for £3.
How much money did the shop collect from the pears sold on Tuesday and Wednesday?

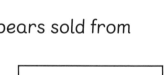

44 Ruby mixed $\frac{3}{5}$ kg of red-coloured sand, $\frac{2}{5}$ kg of green-coloured sand and $\frac{4}{5}$ kg of blue-coloured sand together in a bowl.

The mass of the bowl was $\frac{1}{5}$ kg.

What was the total mass of the bowl and the sand?

45 Charles spent £20.55 at a shop.

He bought a bag and another item at half the marked price.

What was the item he bought at half of the marked price?